I1026615

The Feminist Companion to the Bible
(Second Series)

4

Editor
Athalya Brenner

Sheffield Academic Press

Judges

A Feminist Companion to the Bible
(Second Series)

edited by Athalya Brenner

BS
1305.2
.J820
1999

Copyright © 1999 Sheffield Academic Press

Published by Sheffield Academic Press Ltd
Mansion House
19 Kingfield Road
Sheffield, S11 9AS
England

Printed on acid-free paper in Great Britain
by The Cromwell Press
Trowbridge, Wiltshire

British Library Cataloguing in Publication Data

A catalogue record for this book is available
from the British Library

ISBN 1-84127-024-5

JESUIT - KRAUSS - McCORMICK - LIBRARY
1100 EAST 55th STREET
CHICAGO, ILLINOIS 60615

To the memory of

_____

Fokkelien van Dijk-Hemmes

ת•נ•צ•ב•ה•

CONTENTS

ABBREVIATIONS

AB	Anchor Bible
ATD	Das Alte Testament Deutsch
BEAT	Beiträge zur Erforschung des Alten Testaments und des antiken Judentums
BDB	Francis Brown, S.R. Driver and Charles A. Briggs, *A Hebrew and English Lexicon of the Old Testament* (Oxford: Clarendon Press, 1907)
BIS	Biblical Interpretation Series
BR	*Bible Review*
BTB	*Biblical Theology Bulletin*
CBQ	*Catholic Biblical Quarterly*
EvT	*Evangelische Theologie*
FRLANT	Forschungen zur Religion und Literatur des Alten und Neuen Testaments
HeyJ	*Heythrop Journal*
JK	*Junge Kirche*
JSHRZ	Jüdische Schriften aus hellenistisch-römischer Zeit
JSOT	*Journal for the Study of the Old Testament*
JSOTSup	*Journal for the Study of the Old Testament*, Supplement Series
KHAT	Kurzer Hand-Kommentar zum Alten Testament
KJV	King James Version
NEB	Neue Echter Bibel
OBO	Orbis biblicus et orientalis
OTG	Old Testament Guides
OTM	Old Testament Message
OTP	James Charlesworth (ed.), *Old Testament Pseudepigrapha*
RHS	Religionsunterricht an höheren Schulen
SBLDS	SBL Dissertation Series
TOTC	Tyndale Old Testament Commentaries
TRE	*Theologische Realenzyklopädie*
TTZ	*Trierer theologische Zeitschrift*
VT	*Vetus Testamentum*
ZDPV	*Zeitschrift des deutschen Palästina-Vereins*

CONTRIBUTORS

Alice Bach, Case Western University

Athalya Brenner, Department of Theology and Religious Studies, Faculty of the Humanities, University of Amsterdam, Oude Turfmarkt 147, 1012 GC Amsterdam, The Netherlands.

Renate Jost, Oeserstr. 3, D-65934 Frankfurt, Germany.

Lillian R. Klein, 7108 Millwood Road, Bethesda, MD 20817, USA.

Phyllis Silverman Kramer, 6848 Palmetto Circle South Apt. 1215, Boca Raton, FL 33433, USA.

Ilse Müllner, Department 1 (Philosophy, Religious Studies and Social Science/Catholic Theology), University of Essen, Universitätsstr. 2, D-45141, Germany.

Claudia Rakel, Stuehmeyerstr. 10, D-44787 Bochum, Germany.

Carol Smith, Regent's Park College, Oxford, OX1 2LB, England.

Shulamit Valler, Department of Jewish History, University of Haifa, Mt Carmel, Haifa 31999, Israel.

INTRODUCTION

Athalya Brenner

I

There *is* an apparent centrality of women in Judges. Apparent, since a closer examination of the texts may yield the conclusion that the women stories they contain are, by and large, androcentric. Out of 19 female figures or collective figures, only four are named and the others are nameless. Such namelessness can be variously interpreted but, ultimately, hardly seems to indicate complementary centrality. The women are mostly defined by their M [Male/Masculine] relational status: this is a complementary status. They are often presented as social others or outsiders. The textual authority seems to be mostly M, and to argue to the contrary in at least some stories (such as chapters 4 and 5) or as a matter of authorship is not easy. Violence against women is routinely considered or committed, probably as an extended hyperbole symbolic of the disintegrating social order.

These observations appear in my 'Introduction' to the first *Feminist Companion to Judges*, published in 1993.[1] I think that they are still valid now, six years later. Feminist critics are still greatly preoccupied with the places and socio-literary roles of F [Female/Feminine) figurations in Judges. The problem of violence continues to be confronted, again and again. But the tone has subtly changed, as has the agenda. Instead of mainly looking for signs of and tracing victimization, attempts are made to reread F figurations in new ways. M figurations are being reconsidered as well. The question of the body, especially but not only the gendered body, receives a lot of attention. There is an ever-growing interest in intertextuality, inside and outside the biblical writings; and in the significance of Judges for the social and anthropological analyses of gender relations in the biblical worlds of words and outside them. The feminist dialogue now looks inwards and back,

---

1. A. Brenner (ed.), *A Feminist Companion to Judges* (The Feminist Companion to the Bible, 4; Sheffield: Sheffield Academic Press, 1993), pp. 9-22.

building on recent feminist work (beginning in the 1970s but prolif-
erating in the 1990s) in biblical criticism and interpretation as well as
outside biblical studies, and drawing from the large body of accumu-
lated feminist research in the Humanities and the Social Sciences.

Most of the recent work on Judges, including feminist work, is well
known, translated into several languages and largely quoted—and
discussed—in individual articles. It also appears in the composite Bibliography at the end of this volume. Hence, it will not be mentioned
here. Two exceptions, however, will be made. One is the significant
contribution of works by Mieke Bal (see Bibliography). The other is the
English translation of Yairah Amit's important monograph on Judges
which, it is hoped, will be available to readers by the time this volume
goes to press.[2] Amit's book, although not ostensibly 'feminist' in its
approach, will undoubtedly be of help to all readers of Judges.

It is therefore preferable, I think, to view this volume as a continuation of as well as progress upon of the first Judges volume. Readers
will surely note the changes in tone and method, especially since several of the articles were implicitly written in dialogue with previous
Feminist Companion articles.

II

Unlike the practice in previous volumes, the articles included in this
one are arranged in the order of the biblical text—from ch. 1 through
to ch. 21—each article chiefly relates to.

In her article 'A Spectrum of Female Characters in the Book of Judges' Lillian Klein wrote briefly about Achsah (ch. 1), defining her as 'a
role model of propriety for later portrayals of women'.[3] In 'Achsah:
What Price this Prize?', Klein revisits Achsah's story to develop her
short observation further. She shows how Achsah, although resorting
to stereotyped F wiles, wins her ends as well as succeeds in mediating
the functions of daughter and wife that some of other F figurations in
Judges do not manage. Therefore, Achsah is an object of admiration
and indeed an F (and named) model, although she remains a relational male-model.

---

2.   Y. Amit, *The Book of Judges: The Art of Editing* (Leiden: E.J. Brill, 1999;
translated from the Hebrew). See also Amit's article, ' "Manoah Promptly Followed
his Wife" (Judges 13.11): On the Place of the Woman in Birth Narratives', in Brenner (ed.), *A Feminist Companion to Judges*, pp. 146-56.
3.   In Brenner (ed.), *A Feminist Companion to Judges*, pp. 24-33 (25).

Claudia Rakel aims 'to show the intertextual relations' between Judith's hymn in Jdt. 16.1-17 and two other biblical poems the text ascribes to women—Judg. 5.2-31 and Exod. 15.1-19. Therefore her article, '"I will Sing a New Song to my God": Some Remarks on the Intertextuality of Judith 16.1-17', is included here. After a brief discussion of intertextuality as a hermeneutic approach, Rakel moves on to consider the Greek versions of the three texts she reads together. Section 3 of her article is a comparison between the song of Deborah and Judith's song: both structure and contents are here analyzed. She views Judith's song as a continuation of the tradition represented by Judges 5. A comparison of Judith 16 and Exodus 15 is followed by a discussion of the Judith text as against its 'models'.

Two articles take Jephthah's daughter, the nameless relational figure who agrees to be sacrificed to YHWH by her father in Judges 11, as the subject for intertextual readings. In both, Jewish interpretations are read alongside the biblical story. However, Valler discusses the earlier materials while Kramer chooses to read later Jewish commentary together with some artworks.

In 'The Story of Jephthah's Daughter in the Midrash', Shulamit Valler traces the discomfort of the Jewish sages with this terrifying story. Their solution is to displace the responsibility for this tragedy from the daughter (according to Jephthah, 11.35) and the god who allowed the vow and its consequences, to Jephthah himself. Jephthah is wholly mistaken in his attitude and assumptions: it is left for his god to view Jephthah's dilemma with sorrow and regret.

In 'Jephthah's Daughter: A Thematic Approach to the Narrative as Seen in Selected Rabbinic Exegesis and in Artwork', Phyllis Silverman Kramer distinguishes three themes in the biblical story: Jephthah's daughter greeting her father upon his arrival home; the daughter lamenting her maidenhood with her friends; and the sacrifice of the daughter. She then discusses these three themes as they appear in the HB and then recycled in two disparate types of intertexts: the interpretation of the story in rabbinic and later traditional Jewish exegesis; and in some examples of European art (reproductions of the discussed artworks are included). An Appendix at the end of Kramer's article lists additional artworks on the daughter and her father, again arranged in the same thematic groups.

Two articles, by Smith and by Jost, discuss stories from the Samson cycle or, more precisely, Samson's encounter with Delilah and its aftermath (Judges 16).

Carol Smith asks, is 'Delilah: A Suitable Case for (Feminist) Treatment?' Why is Delilah so fascinating for readers, why are the interpretations of her story so different from each other, even among feminist readers? Smith traces such differences to the changes in the ongoing project of feminist Bible criticism and its shifting agendas. She leads us through a tour of recent feminist writings on this story, and concludes: 'Whether Delilah was delicious, delightful and delectable or deceitful, despicable and debauched—or maybe all of these—is for us all to decide for ourselves. I only ask that we listen to each other while deciding, and, even if we do not return completely to our feminist roots, at least remember them'.

'God of Love/God of Vengeance, Or Samson's '"Prayer for Vengeance"', by Renate Jost, relates to another section of Judges 16—the story of Samson's prayer (v. 28) and his death. Her interest is theological, but also social. Jost discusses the relevant works by Ebach and Zenger concerning the claim often made that the god of the HB is a god of vengeance, whereas the god of the NT is a god of love and mercy. Jost argues that examining the paternal, rather than patriarchal, world of the Bible is feminist work. Proceeding from this position, and building on Ebach and Zenger's work, she applies it to Samson's prayer and to his story in general. Through a philological analysis and a review of interpretations on the passage, she offers alternative feminist options for reading the story, and concludes that 'the faith in the God of love as also a God of vengeance is indispensable even for a Christian feminist understanding of love'.

The last two articles in this collection are on the so-called second appendix to the book of Judges, the narrative of the rape in Gibeah and its public consequences (Judg. 19–21). Müllner reads ch. 19, Bach reads ch. 21. Both examine the significance of sexual violence against women. In both a next-generation approach, clearly discernible from the 'defining the victim of patriarchy' approach of the 1970s and the early 1980s feminist criticism, is clearly discernible.

In 'Lethal Differences: Sexual Violence as Violence against Others in Judges 19', Ilse Müllner begins by discussing feminist attitudes to sexual violence and classism, then moves on to analyse (white, European/Western) feminist racism in general and anti-Judaism in particular. The urgent feminist need to focus on sexual violence against women cannot cancel out feminism's need to apply to other processes of excluding Others—on the basis of race, or colour, or class, or religion. After discussing anti-Judaic tendency in feminist treatments of sexual violence, Müllner proceeds to read the story of Judges 19–20, the Wife's story in Gibeah, as an account of male search for self and identity by the negation and destruction of the Other.

Alice Bach, in 'Reading the Body Politic: Women, Violence and Judges 21', powerfully begins by asserting: 'Rape is a weapon. Rape is a weapon to reassert the power of a man over an enemy. Rape is used to create fear in women'. Bach builds on work by Bal, Exum, Niditch and others to create a literary strategy that would make approaching the collective rape story (ch. 21) possible to comprehend. The young women of Shiloh are captured, taken. Readers do not usually comment that they are also raped. Throughout it all, the young women remain not only nameless but also decidedly silent. The biblical text silences them, mutes them, absolutely. Bach therefore urges readers at least to acknowledge the literary rape. She also supplies the muted young women with a voice—the contemporary analogous voice of young Bosnian women, 'taken' in war and raped. By following this strategy Bach practises the primary feminist credo of involvement in social situations, in Academe as well as outside it.[4]

4.   I would like to thank Derek Suchard, of Amsterdam, who greatly assisted me in the technical aspects of editing this volume.

ACHSAH: WHAT PRICE THIS PRIZE?

Lillian R. Klein

In the first *Feminist Companion to Judges,* my article entitled 'A Spectrum of Female Characters in the Book of Judges'[1] introduces Achsah 'as a role model of propriety for later portrayals of women' in the book.[2] The brevity (Judg. 1.12-15) and density of Achsah's portrayal, however, suggest the text may have much more to say about her. My objective here is to explore and discover more about the woman I have read as as an ideal of womanhood in Judges.

Achsah appears in two (almost identical) texts: in Joshua 15 and in Judges 1. In the former, Achsah is one of only two women to be identified in the book: Raḥab (Josh. 2.1-21) is the *zônāh* (innkeeper, prostitute) of Jericho who recognizes YHWH as 'Elohim in the heavens above and on the earth below', and Achsah (Josh. 15.16-19) is a daughter of the Kenites given by her father as a prize to a brave warrior. In Judges (1.12-15), Achsah is the first woman to be mentioned in the book which introduces more individual women than any other book in the Hebrew Bible. Achsah is thus both a balance for one other woman, in Joshua, and the initial woman of a remarkable series of (remarkable, in one way or another) women, in Judges. The first consideration is whether the contexts in which Achsah is placed in these two narratives shed any light on who she is.

In Joshua, Raḥab is an innkeeper-prostitute, a woman whose profession it is to actively engage with men as an independent agent for her own monetary benefit. Initially, Raḥab seems a counterbalance to Achsah, the dutiful daughter who is given by her father as a prize to a brave warrior. But interesting similarities interfere with such simple opposition. Both women are non-Israelite by birth—Raḥab a citizen of

---

1.   Lillian R. Klein, 'A Spectrum of Female Characters in the Book of Judges', in A. Brenner (ed.), *A Feminist Companion to Judges* (The Feminist Companion to the Bible, 4; Sheffield: Sheffield Academic Press: 1993), pp. 24-33.
2.   Klein, 'Spectrum', p. 25.

Jericho and Achsah a descendent of Jethro,[3] the Midianite priest who was Moses' father-in-law. Furthermore both women, foreigners by birth and at opposite ends of the social scale, recognize YHWH as the supreme deity.[4] The complex comparison of the women in Joshua alerts the reader to possible complexities in the presentation of Achsah in Judges. But before we turn to see what information Judges provides on who Achsah is, let us consider more closely the narrative environment in which she is presented.[5]

Both Joshua and Judges are concerned with the occupation of the land. Thus, in both books, the milieu of Achsah's story is essentially the same. The book of Judges opens to a world of men's concerns, primarily war and occupation. The first eleven verses describe the battles of Judah and Simeon to conquer Judah's lot, or allotted portion of Canaan. Judah and Simeon lead a series of aggressive expeditions against various native peoples who live in Jerusalem,[6] in the mountains, in the Negev and in the foothills (1.8-9). Except for occasional names of conquered enemy leaders, only Judah and Simeon have been identified as warriors. Suddenly, from this wide-angle point of view, the text moves in close to present individual characters in a specific situation. From this point, the narrative proceeds with such speed and compression it evokes Erich Auerbach's description of biblical style: undefined but heavily present background and suggested depths of meaning.[7]

Judah has advanced upon a community called Devir (formerly Kiryat Sepher). The text calls our attention to the town under attack by giving it two names, present and past. The earlier name, Kiryat Sepher, suggests 'City of the Book' or 'City of Scribes', whereas Devir alludes to the back area, the most holy part of a temple, hence a 'Holy City'.

3.   Jethro is named Re'uel and his land and priesthood are identified as Midianite in Exod. 2.16. 'Kenite' may be used in this passage to differentiate this group identified with the Israelites from the Midianites with whom they will do battle in subsequent chapters.

4.   Fewell and Gunn discuss Raḥab's possibile motivations in Danna Nolan Fewell and David M. Gunn, *Gender, Power and Promise: The Subject of the Bible's First Story* (Nashville: Abingdon Press, 1993), pp. 117-21.

5.   Because the Joshua and Judges texts are essentially repetitive, I will rely on the Judges text.

6.   See my discussion in *The Triumph of Irony in the Book of Judges* (JSOTSup, 68; Bible and Literature, 14; Sheffield: Sheffield Academic Press, 1988), p. 25.

7.   Erich Auerbach, *Mimesis: The Representation of Reality in Western Literature* (trans. Willard Trask; New York: New York University Press, 1953), pp. 12-13.

Devir has also been called a 'royal city of the Canaanites'.[8] In Joshua, Devir is called *Kiryat Šānāh*, 'city of instruction'.[9] At the outset this is a significant conquest for the Israelites, for they attack not only territory but also a seat of foreign rule and religious beliefs.[10]

Suddenly, a new character speaks: Caleb promises his daughter as wife[11] to the one who attacks and captures Kiryath Sepher—referring to the city by its ancient, probably more hallowed title. The speaker, Caleb, is identified in this text[12] not as an Israelite from Egypt but as a Kenite, a descendant of Jethro, the Kenite priest and father-in-law of Moses (1.16).[13] The Kenites had been faithful to the Israelite's cause throughout their passage in the desert, and Judges describes them as having recently traveled and, presumably, fought with Judah from the City of Palms to the wilderness of Judah, south of Arad (1.16). The Kenites have recognized YHWH as the supreme divinity;[14] they may be called, in a variation of modern parlance, 'Israelites by Choice'. Their being identified as Kenites, however, suggests that they are traveling as a separate group within the larger Israelite community. In this text, the Kenites seem to be associated with respect. We note that Caleb apparently enjoys some prestige since he can offer his daughter as a prize to the man who captures the city.

No mention has yet been made in Judges of booty taking, which is specifically forbidden (Deut. 20.13),[15] but Caleb's statement obliquely alludes to that practice. His daughter, we note, is a prize for con-

---

8.   Francis Brown, S.R. Driver and Charles A. Briggs, *The New Brown–Driver–Gesenius Hebrew–Aramaic Lexicon* (BDB, n.d.; repr. Christian Copyrights, n.p. 1983).

9.   H. Friedman's translation, 'Joshua: An Introduction and Commentary', in A. Cohen (ed.), *Joshua and Judges* (Hindhead, Surrey: Soncino, 1959), p. 89.

10.   Fewell bemoans the loss of culture that results from the conquest of such a center of learning, in 'Deconstructive Criticism: Achsah and the (E)razed City of Writing', in Gale A. Yee (ed.), *Judges and Method: New Approaches in Biblical Studies*, (Minneapolis: Fortress Press, 1995), pp. 131-32.

11.   Intertextual reading offers an ironic comparison with Saul's offer of his daughter Merab to David for fighting the Philistines. Saul's objective, however, is to have the Philistines kill David. 1 Sam. 18.17.

12.   In Num. 13.6 Caleb is identified as a Judahite, the son of Jephunneh. In Judges, however, Caleb is repeatedly identified as a Kenite. Elsewhere, Caleb's connection to Judah is not emphasized, only his descent from Jephunneh.

13.   And Achsah is not a descendant of Sarah in this text, as Fewell seems to take for granted. Fewell and Gunn, *Gender*, p. 122.

14.   Exod. 18.11: 'And Jethro said, "Now I know that YHWH (is) greater than all the gods"'.

15.   Cf. also Gen. 34, where Dinah's brothers do take booty after revenging themselves for her rape.

quering a town, which anticipates and obviates the common practice of taking the women of conquered peoples as booty—at least for one man. Not only does a daughter of the people offered as a prize make foreign women less desirable, but a woman of the Israelites is elevated compared to the humiliation of women taken as spoil. I read the text as implying that this daughter—an emblem of daughters of Israel —is a woman to be valued.

The fact that a Kenite woman, identified as such, is offered as a paradigm for Israelite womanhood invites consideration. It is unlikely that the text is suggesting that no Israelite woman is ideal. Instead, the text uses a sub-group of the Israelite company to make a statement about the ideal qualities projected for the larger community—men and women alike. I submit that by focusing on Caleb and the Kenites, the text suggests that converts to Israelite beliefs and practices may be more sincere and devoted in their adherence to those traditions than those who are merely born into the faith and accept their heritage without question.[16] Because some texts identify Caleb as a Judahite,[17] his persistent identification in this text as a Kenite reinforces this view of foreign devotees of YHWH. This is consonant with the sympathetic portrayal of Raḥab in Joshua but contradictory to later portrayals of foreign women—who do not accept YHWH— in Judges.[18]

However, if Achsah is a model for Israelite womanhood, what is the text suggesting about model womanhood? Is she a prize, like an object, for male deeds of heroism? That she is *given* implies that the image of Israelite-woman-as-prize is one of docile subordination to male-dominated authority. Such nuances contribute to fleshing out a picture of Achsah-as-woman in this text.

Not only does Caleb offer his daughter as wife to the conqueror, but he immediately identifies her by name: Achsah. Being named or unnamed is significant in Biblical texts, and the fact that Caleb's daughter is immediately named grants her further substance. Her name, possibly derived from *'ēkes*, 'anklet', 'bangle', is alluringly sexy or at the very least evokes a playful quality. At this point in the text Achsah is perceived as a lure, a decoration, a sexy embellishment, a toy given to the bravest man around.

---

16. Achsah and Ruth share these qualities.

17. See Num. 13.6.

18. Indeed, the subsequent women in Judges read in this light offer a panorama of acceptable/non-acceptable females, and the key to acceptability is based not on birth but on acceptance of YHWH. See Klein, 'Spectrum', pp. 24-33.

No sooner does Caleb make his offer than his own nephew warrants the prize. The text states that Othniel, son of Caleb's younger brother Kenaz, is victor over Kiryath Sepher. It is impossible to determine how broadly Caleb's offer was disseminated—whether, for instance, the Judahites even knew of it. It seems likely that Caleb's action and Othniel's victory was a local transaction as part of the larger invasion, that separate camps of the Judahite forces went out on independent sorties as part of the general mission. This reinforces the idea that the Kenites are travelling as an independent group alongside, rather than intermingled with, the Judahites.

With Othniel's victory, Caleb forthwith completes his side of the bargain: he gives Achsah to Othniel as wife. Immediately, the text shifts to more intense compression and picks up tempo; in fact the marriage, however it was performed, is subsumed. The narrative continues with 'And it was', *wayyᵉhî*, to introduce a new phase of the action, moving from the social to the personal aspect of the narrative. Thus in only two verses the text has sharpened its focus from all the sons of Judah to Caleb and the Kenites and, beginning with *wayyᵉhî*, to the personal world of the bridal pair.

Furthermore, 'And it was' introduces more than a narrower focus. With this phrase, the text shifts from a male perspective to that of a female: from Caleb and the Kenites to Achsah, the bride; from war and death to land and water and generation. Whereas the former male action is neither immediate nor described, Achsah is suddenly present. She is introduced, as it were, in motion: 'As she came' (1.14). The cause and effect mode of the initial masculine-dominated verses is replaced by specific and more intense action. Indeed, Achsah is depicted doing two things simultaneously or at least interdependently.

The text has it that Achsah '*incites* (root: *syt* in the hiphil) him to ask for a field from her father'(1.14).[19] This is a troubling verse on several accounts. One problem is the identity of the masculine pronoun, which has no antecedent. It has usually been assumed that Achsah interacts with Othniel to ask her father, in which case we have the bride *inciting* or *provoking* her husband, which introduces a possibly

19. This reading supports rather than deviates from the Masoretic text ('And it happened as she came and she incited him to ask from her father...'). Compare the Septuagint and Vulgate 'corrections' of the text: 'and she came and he persuaded her to ask', altered so that 'the request does not come from Achsah' (C.F. Burney, *The Book of Judges* [New York: Ktav, 1970 (1903, 1918)], p. 13), or 'to preserve the image of the first savior judge' (R.G. Boling, *Judges: A New Translation with Introduction and Commentary* [AB, 6A; Garden City, NY: Doubleday, 1975], p. 57).

negative connotation to her actions.[20] We can understand the negative connotation suggested in the English translation of 'incites', but the contradiction between this negative connotation and the positive aspects of her actions creates a tension in the text. I will return to the connotations of Achsah's actions. I shall first consider to whom she is speaking.

One reading suggests not Othniel but Caleb, Achsah's father, is the object of the bride's importuning.[21] In this reading, Achsah 'beguiles' her father, asking her father directly for the land. Here the negative connotation is accepted as alluding to the ill Achsah does her father through his 'quite real loss of two valuable sources of water'.[22] This reading, which has the young bride using manipulation to take advantage of her own father, seems strained and unconvincing. Achsah, I will assume, speaks to her husband.

At this juncture, I note, Achsah goes about her business unhesitatingly. She knows what is important in her world. That she incites her husband to make the request rather than ask her father herself suggests feminine restraint and shame,[23] leaving the important transactions to the men—attributes valued in biblical womanhood.[24]

Whether Achsah incites or beguiles, modern interpretations have Achsah being manipulative—either of her husband or her father. On the other hand, the word need not be negative in this situation, implying instead the woman's energy and intelligence. If she is manipulating Othniel, is he left standing stupidly on the side, as has been assumed,[25] or does his implied acquiescence signal he is responding positively to her suggestion? Is a man who accedes to his wife's importuning necessarily a dunce or could he be a smart partner who recognizes the value of his wife's suggestion, much as Adam responded to Eve? After all, Achsah is in a better position to be privy to her father's circumstances than Othniel is, and her suggestion may reflect this insider knowledge. That she *incites* her husband may reflect the energy she feels constrained to use in this male-dominated culture.

20. Paul G. Mosca, 'Who Seduced Whom? A Note on Joshua 15:18//Judges 1.14', *CBQ* 45.1 (1984), pp. 18-22 (18-19).

21. Mosca, 'Who Seduced Whom?', pp. 18-22.

22. Mosca, 'Who Seduced Whom?', p. 22.

23. See my discussion in 'Honor and Shame in Esther', in A. Brenner (ed.), *A Feminist Companion to Esther, Judith and Susanna* (The Feminist Companion to the Bible, 7; Sheffield: Sheffield Academic Press: 1995), pp. 149-75.

24. The biblical matriarchs certainly do not participate in worldly affairs. Sarah is even rebuked for laughing to herself at what she overhears (Gen. 18.10).

25. Mosca, 'Who Seduced Whom?', p. 19.

And is not manipulation one of the few ways in which women can achieve what they know to be best for all concerned—a means recognized and accepted by male and female alike? Perhaps our modern disdain for the term is inappropriately applied. Accordingly, I shall use 'manipulation' without censure to refer to Achsah's actions.

However, Achsah's modest demeanor in urging *her husband* to do the asking is at odds with the decisiveness she demonstrates by inciting her husband—*even as she comes to him* as a bride. There is even a suggestion of sexual moment in Achsah's request: she asks 'as she comes'; and the verb 'come' may allude to sexual intercourse. The verb translated as *incite* actually bridges two actions: *as she came* and *to ask for a field from her father*, which links Achsah's arrival/sex and her request. Thus Achsah may be seen as engaging her husband in decision making at a moment in which he is most likely to be psychologically malleable. We may view this as manipulative, but the text does not judge her actions negatively.

In any event, Achsah's initial action erodes the earlier masculine image of a prize woman as a passive, decorative bangle. In her actions, Achsah immediately comes across as smart and determined, as someone who knows how to operate within the constraints of society. Furthermore, her being active does not make her husband passive any more than her intelligence makes him stupid. Indeed, Othniel's passivity would hardly accord with his military prowess. The text could just as likely be showing Othniel's intelligence and willingness to act by accepting his wife's suggestion about approaching her father and acting upon it. Elsewhere, biblical texts praise women who are wise and bring their husbands the benefits of their intelligent actions.[26]

In the same verse, without transition, the text moves abruptly to present the consequences of the initial clause of the sentence. The text presenting only essential information, Othniel's actual request of Caleb, and Caleb's actual granting of a land parcel to the newlyweds are subsumed. In this second action of the sentence, Achsah is depicted as prostrating herself before her father. Achsah's arrival before her father and even her alighting from her donkey are suppressed [27] and only her prostration before Caleb is conveyed by the verb *tiṣnaḥ*, 'dropped down'. As I have observed elsewhere, 'the Hebrew is so concentrated it almost sounds like Achsah falls off her donkey before her father. That she gets down from her donkey is unimportant; what

26. Cf. Ruth and the poem in Prov. 31.10-31.
27. An interesting suppression of two male actions balanced by two overt female actions.

matters is that she shows her father utmost respect, "dropping down" before him'.[28]

With this phrase the narrative moves a final step toward immediate, dramatized action, a tight focus on what began just three verses ago in panoramic vision. In measured, incremental phases, the text has moved from narrative of Judahite action to narrated discourse focusing on Caleb and the Kenites, to this apex in direct discourse between Achsah and Caleb. The narrative achieves closure in the last phrase by returning to narrated action.

Achsah's dramatized interaction with her father, we note, is in an entirely different mode than her earlier narrated action with her husband—supporting the view that her earlier action was *not* with her father. Here she is supplicant; with Othniel she was manipulative, taking advantage of a sexual situation, determined. This third perspective of Achsah—sexy toy, manipulative woman, prostrate and supplicant daughter—suggests a new complexity to the text and our understanding of Achsah.

Achshah's prostrating herself before her father is a clear signal to him that she wants something. His immediate response is, 'What to you?' or 'What do you want?' Achsah's resorting to a culturally established means of establishing communication with her father may suggest that her approach to her husband is also culturally entrenched, that the sexual moment is an appropriate moment for broaching a woman's desires.

At this point, what Achsah wants from her father is twofold—or two aspects of one desire. Still in direct speech, she says, 'Give me a blessing. Since you have given me land of the Negev, give me springs of water'. In asking for a blessing, Achsah evokes the blessings given to sons in Genesis.[29] Since Caleb and his family are Kenites, the allusion to intertextual blessing seems to be reinforcing the textual acceptance of these people, a foreign people welcome to Israelite tradition. By placing Achsah in this perspective, the text reinforces that daughters also be recognized as inheritors of tradition, of family.[30] The recognition Achsah asks for and Caleb gives, however, is not the kind of verbal prophecy found in Genesis. It is tangible, sources of water to make their arid land arable. The word 'blessing' evokes intertextual

---

28. Klein, *Triumph of Irony*, p. 26.

29. Beginning with God's blessing of Isaac (Gen. 25.11) and continuing with Isaac's blessing of Jacob and Esau (Gen. 27.15-40), Jacob's blessing of his sons and grandsons (chs. 48–49).

30. Established in Num. 27.7.

associations, and its use in this context adds another element of meaning to the word.

Achsah may also be asking for the blessing only women can realize, the blessing of life, of birth. In asking for water for the land Caleb has given her, Achsah is likening herself to the land, a place for planting seed. Caleb has given both Achsah and land—both places for planting seed—to Caleb in marriage. Now, Achsah asks, give me the necessary water of life to permit seeds to grow.

Thus the three separate references to Achsah—as prize, as bride and as daughter—all allude to sex, and in different ways. As a prize, Achsah is seen a sex toy; as a bride, Achsah uses sex to gain land to live on; and as a dutiful daughter, Achsah uses her sexual capacity to reproduce to gain water to make that land and her life viable. Achsah is a vital woman who knows how to live within the constraints of her society, who recognizes what is important to her in that social milieu, and who acts decisively, adjusting method to the situation at hand.

And the text admires her. Certainly written from a male perspective, this text describes an ideal woman for all Israelite women to emulate. The sex-kitten-prize does not obviate admiration for a woman who knows when her husband is weakest and uses it—not to take advantage of him (as Delilah does) but to enrich them both. And the daughter who inveigles her father to give her the means to give him grandchildren is rewarded by getting not only one spring but two—her request has surely met parental approval.

Achsah is a complex woman, but the overriding factor which makes her an ideal woman is not even mentioned in the text: acceptance of YHWH. Achsah is a Kenite, and the Kenites have 'wholly followed YHWH'.[31] That Achsah is a follower of YHWH is subsumed in this text. The sex kitten who does *not* adhere to YHWH is the dangerous Delilah. But being faithful to YHWH is not sufficient to make a woman a role model. Jael, who uses sex to kill is *not* identified as a mother, and the submissive daughter who is *not* intelligent and decisive is Jepthah's daughter, sacrificed to her father's rash vow. Women, the text suggests, should use all their capacities—(implicit) faith, procreative sex, and decisive intelligence (aka manipulation)—to live what the patriarchs deemed rich lives for women.

31. Klein, 'Spectrum', pp. 24-33.

'I WILL SING A NEW SONG TO MY GOD': SOME REMARKS ON THE INTERTEXTUALITY OF JUDITH 16.1-17[*]

Claudia Rakel

The book of Judith contains many allusions to other biblical texts. The fictitious novel, which is of late composition,[1] does not make any historical event the centerpiece of the narrative, but is rather an amalgamation of various historical events, weaving the strands of different biblical traditions into a many-hued, complex narrative. There is apparently nothing that is not already known from other biblical texts: an argument between YHWH and Nebuchadnezzar that is structurally similar to the one between YHWH and Pharaoh (Exod.);[2] the head of an enemy leader (2 Macc. 15);[3] a woman who, on the one hand, saves Israel by killing this leader (Judg. 4–5),[4] and, on the other hand, plucks up courage and uses her beauty to achieve her aims, although doing so means risking her life (Est. 5);[5] a people whose faith in the God of Israel is shaken by lack of water (Exod. 17.1-8; Num. 2.2-13; Deut. 33.8-11);[6] a festival at whose head stand the women of Israel and during which they sing a song of triumph (Exod. 15.20–21; 1 Sam. 18.6-

---

[*]   Translated by Stefanie Bloch, Kathrin Huewe and Robert Nusbaum.

1.   Most exegetes accept c. 100 BCE as the date of composition.

2.   Cf. E. Zenger, *Das Buch Judit* (JSHRZ, 1; Gütersloh: Gütersloher Verlagshaus, 1981), pp. 445-46.

3.   Cf. Zenger, *Buch Judit*, p. 443.

4.   Cf. S.A. White, 'In the Steps of Jael and Deborah: Judith as Heroine', in J.C. VanderKam (ed.), *'No One Spoke Ill of Her': Essays on Judith* (SBL Early Judaism and its Literature, 2; Atlanta: Scholars Press, 1992), pp. 5-16.

5.   Cf. M. Hellmann, *Judit—eine Frau im Spannungsfeld von Autonomie und göttlicher Führung: Studie über eine Frauengestalt des Alten Testaments* (Frankfurt am Main: Peter Lang, 1992), p. 109; see also T. Craven, 'Tradition and Convention in the Book of Judith', in A. Loades (ed.), *Feminist Theology: A Reader* (Louisville, KY: Westminster/John Knox Press, 1990), pp. 29-41.

6.   Cf. J.W. van Henten, 'Judith as Alternative Leader: A Rereading of Judith 7–13', in A. Brenner (ed.), *A Feminist Companion to Esther, Judith and Susanna* (The Feminist Companion to the Bible, 7; Sheffield: Sheffield Academic Press, 1995), pp. 224-52.

7);[7] a woman who, like Delilah, uses beauty and deceit to cast a spell over and destroy the enemy leader (Judg. 16).[8] And this list could easily be continued. It almost seems as though the book of Judith were trying to touch upon the whole biblical tradition. At least the assessment that the narrative is 'a goldmine for readers looking for possible quotations and allusions'[9] cannot be rejected.

The passage discussed below (Jdt. 16.1-17), in which Judith, at the end of the book, sings a song of praise to YHWH because he has freed his people, could also be added to the above list. This is not the only narrative passage in the Bible containing a hymn-like song that praises God for saving his people Israel: Judges 5 and Exodus 15 also contain such songs, which recapitulate previously narrated events and ascribe them to God. Like Judith's, these songs tell of YHWH's marvelous deeds on Israel's behalf,[10] and weave into the texture of the narrative thanks to him for his intervention.[11] The events described in the texts from which the three songs are taken all recount YHWH's saving Israel from a threat, and the Israelite's subsequent expression of joy in the form of a hymn. Thus, the songs' literary function is close to that of a 'metatext', a kind of retrospective commentary, a backward look at the entire narrative. Although many previous studies[12] have pointed out that Jdt. 16.1-17 'is especially close to other songs of triumph, especially that of Deborah and Barak after Jael had killed Sisera (Judg. 5) and that of Moses and Miriam after the crossing of the Red Sea (Exod. 15)',[13] there have to date been few detailed comparative studies of the songs themselves.[14]

7.   Regarding biblical texts in which women sing songs of praise, see E.B. Poethig, 'The Victory Song Tradition of the Women of Israel' (PhD dissertation, New York University, 1985).

8.   Cf. B. Merideth, 'Desire and Danger: The Drama of Betrayal in Judges and Judith', in M. Bal (ed.), *Anti-Covenant: Counter-Reading Women's Lives in the Hebrew Bible* (Sheffield: Almond Press, 1989), pp. 63-78.

9.   Henten, 'Alternative Leader', p. 224.

10.   Cf. H.-P. Mathys, *Dichter und Beter: Theologen aus spätalttestamentlicher Zeit* (OBO, 132; Freiburg: Universitätsverlag; Göttingen: Vandenhoeck & Ruprecht, 1994), p. 175.

11.   Cf. Mathys, *Dichter und Beter*, p. 176.

12.   Cf., for example, J. Craghan, *Esther, Judith, Tobit, Jonah, Ruth* (OTM, 16; Wilmington, DE: Michael Glazier, 1982), p. 118; C.A. Moore, *Judith: A New Translation with Introduction and Commentary* (AB 40; Garden City, NY: Doubleday, 1985), p. 256.

13.   J.C. Dancy, *The Shorter Books of the Apocrypha* (Cambridge Bible Commentary. New English Bible, 28; Cambridge: Cambridge University Press, 1972), p. 124.

14.   Exceptions to this are Shekan, who analyses Jdt. 16 against the background

The aim of the following analysis is to show the intertextual relationships between Jdt. 16.1-17, Judg. 5.2-31 and Exod. 15.1-19 as far as structure, content and theme are concerned. The intensity of these intertextual relationships reveals the biblical traditions in which the book of Judith positions itself. The feminist interest in such an intertextual reading is to describe Judith as a figure who has links to biblical traditions of women (like the singing of victory songs by Deborah and Miriam) and who even revives the Exodus tradition which originally had a male protagonist, Moses.

1. *Intertextuality as an Interpretive Approach*

Are the many intertextual connections with other biblical texts central to the author's intention and to his fictitious text and thereby an extraordinary characteristic of the book of Judith?[15] Or are we dealing here with a phenomenon which is common to all literary and biblical texts and thus has no specific intention? Between these two questions lies the whole expanse of concepts and theories regarding intertextuality, which will only very briefly be outlined here. Approaches with post-structuralist tendencies begin from the assumption that every text is a reaction to an earlier text, and that this phenomenon constitutes a kind of universal law of texts.[16] Regarding the relationship between author and reader these approaches propose the thesis that the intertextual relations between texts are primarily invented by the reader during the act of reading.[17]

---

of Exod. 15 (P.W. Shekan, 'The Hand of Judith', *CBQ* 25 [1963], pp. 94-110), and Gardner, who comparatively analysed the three songs (A.E. Gardner, 'The Song of Praise in Judith 16, 2-17 [LXX 16, 1-17]', *HeyJ* 29 [1988], pp. 413-22).

15. Unlike Van Henten's article (cf. 'Alternative Leader', p. 225), this one assumes that the book of Judith was written by a male author, primarily because the text chooses a female protagonist who is described mainly from a male point of view: 'Heroines like Esther and Judith fit perfectly into a man-made gallery of ideal feminity' (F. van Dijk-Hemmes, 'Traces of Women's Texts in the Hebrew Bible', in A. Brenner and F. van Dijk-Hemmes, *On Gendering Texts: Female and Male Voices in the Hebrew Bible* [BIS, 1; Leiden: E.J. Brill, 1993], pp. 17-109 [p. 31]). However, it should not be denied that the book of Judith contains elements that sometimes break through its androcentric frame (cf. part 5 below).

16. Cf. M. Pfister, 'Konzepte der Intertextualität', in U. Broich and M. Pfister (eds.), *Intertextualität: Formen, Funktionen, anglistische Fallstudien* (Konzepte der Sprach- und Literaturwissenschaft, 35; Tübingen: Niemeyer, 1985), pp. 1-30, esp. pp. 11-20.

17. Cf. Pfister, 'Intertextualität', pp. 20-24.

Structuralist or hermeneutic approaches to intertextuality, on the other hand, assume that texts contain demonstrable intertextual relationships to specific pre-texts.[18] In these approaches only those texts which an author is consciously, intentionally, and pointedly alluding to, and which the reader is able to recognize as such, fall into the category of pre-text.[19] The underlying assumption of the present text is that intertextuality is not only a striking characteristic of the book of Judith, but also a literary device that is deliberately called into play in it. The intertextual relationships are neither the result of mere chance, nor do they arise from the fact that each text makes references to other texts. This does not mean that the inherent need of each text to make constant reference to others is denied; or to suggest that a text could choose not to refer to other texts. A text can, however, make more or less explicit reference to other texts, doing so with conscious and deliberate intention. This understanding of intertextuality is based on Pfister's model, which tries to mediate between the two approaches and with whose help individual intertextual relationships between texts can be viewed as an actualization of global intertextuality.[20] Pfister has defined six qualitative criteria[21] for judging the intensity of intertextual relationships. These criteria make it possible to characterize and assess the relationships between literary texts in all their rich complexity:

1. *Referentiality* as a criterion for the intensity of intertextual relationships starts out from the distinction between words and texts as elements that are simply used or to which reference can be made: the stronger the referential character to the pre-text, the more powerful the intertextual relationship. For example, a quotation that can smoothly be placed in a new context has less intertextual power than one that calls attention to itself as a quotation.

2. *Communicativity* assesses the communicative relevance of intertextual relationships. A maximum level of communicativity is attained if the author is aware of the intertextual relationships with the pre-text, and if the text makes clear that the recipient is intended to recognize these references.

---

18. Cf. Pfister, 'Intertextualität', pp. 11-20.
19. Cf. Pfister, 'Intertextualität', pp. 20-24.
20. Cf. Pfister, 'Intertextualität', p. 25.
21. Cf. Pfister, 'Intertextualität', pp. 26-30.

3. *Auto-reflexivity* as a criterion for intertextuality is present in a text if an author does not only draw attention to the references in it, but also reflects on her/his text's intertextual determinedness and referentiality within the text itself.[22]

4. *Structurality* examines the syntagmatic integration of the pre-text into the text. Maximum intensity is attained if the pre-text becomes the structural matrix for the text as a whole. Allusions to and indirect quoting or paraphrasing of the pre-text are, however, low in intertextual intensity.

5. *Selectivity* refers to the conciseness of intertextual references. The question is how trenchantly and explicitly elements of the pre-text are taken up. A direct quotation gives rise to a stronger relationship to the pre-text than does a broad and less pointed allusion.

6. *Dialogibility* sheds light on the dialogue between pre-text and text. It inquires into whether and how text and pre-text are engaged in a dialogue by comparing the original and the new context of the texts. A dialogue is established if the difference between the original and the new context becomes obvious through semantic or ideological tensions. Thus, rather than simply affirming the pre-text, the text establishes a critical distance from it.

According to Pfister, intertextuality requires taking into consideration both qualitative and quantitative criteria, for example, the complexity and frequency of intertextual relations.

2. *The Greek Version of the Text*

Starting out from the thesis that the Greek version of the hymn in the book of Judith has the status of an original,[23] the following discussion therefore compares the three texts in their Septuagint version. While most exegetes assume that the Greek version of the text is a

22. Although this criterion is not present for the passages discussed here, it is mentioned in order not to leave the picture incomplete.

23. The analysis of Exod. 15.1-18 is based on the critical edition by Wevers (*Exodus* [ed. J.W. Wevers; Septuagint, II.1; Göttingen: Vandenhoeck & Ruprecht, 1991], pp. 196-202). The analysis of Judg. 5.2–31 is based on the edition by Swete (*Judges* [ed. H.B. Swete; OTG, 1; Cambridge: Cambridge University Press, 1925]), pp. 485-89).

translation of a lost Hebrew original,[24] Zenger[25] and Engel[26] put forward the thesis that the book of Judith, as it has come down to us, is
not in fact a translation, but was originally written in Greek. Particularly Zenger makes specific reference to the book of Judith's 'catch-
word' style:

> The book's individual scenes and paragraphs are linked by a varied
> catchword technique. The catchwords also serve as markers of narrative
> and thematic stress, indicators of deeper levels of meaning in the plot,
> which for the author is a coherent and unified whole.[27]

This literary technique is a clear indication that the text was originally written in Greek. It would be extremely difficult for a translation
to sustain such a complex system of connections with catchwords,
which would also have meant an extensive reworking of the text in
Greek. In fact, it is not Engel's intention even to raise the issue of
whether the text, as he puts it, 'contains biblical subjects and motifs
and perhaps even a complete narrative'.[28] However, especially in its
speeches and prayers, the Greek text drew on a Greek rather than a
Hebrew version, and used authentically Greek stylistic devices rather
than translated ones.[29] The most revealing example of the book of
Judith's appropriating of Septuagint theology and formulations is that
Jdt. 16.1-17 includes a quotation (one of several similar ones) from the

---

24. Cf., for example, M.S. Enslin, *The Book of Judith* (Jewish Apocryphal Literature, 7; Leiden: E.J. Brill, 1972), pp. 39-40; Moore, *Judith*, p. 66.

25. In recent articles, E. Zenger revises his earlier thesis that a Hebrew original
exists (cf. E. Zenger, 'Judith/Judithbuch', in *TRE*, XVII, pp. 404-408 [p. 407];
E. Zenger, "Wir erkennen keinen anderen als Gott an..." [Jdt. 8,20]: Programm und
Relevanz des Buches Judith', *RHS* 39.1 [1996], pp. 23-36 [35 n. 1]).

26. Cf. H. Engel, '"Der HERR ist ein Gott, der die Kriege zerschlägt": Zur
griechischen Originalsprache und der Struktur des Buches Judith', in K.-D. Schunck
and M. Augustin (eds.), *Goldene Äpfel in silbernen Schalen* (BEAT, 20; Frankfurt au
Main: Lang, 1992), pp. 155-68.

27. Zenger, *Buch Judit*, p. 433.

28. Engel, 'Der HERR ist ein Gott', p. 156.

29. H. Engel, 'Das Buch Judith', in E. Zenger (ed.), *Einleitung in das Alte Testament* (Stuttgart: Kohlhammer, 1995), pp. 192-200 (197). Because the book of Judith
is quite familiar with Hellenistic sources, H.Y. Priebatsch is of the opinion that the
belief in an original version in Hebrew is hardly verifiable. He also believes that the
text was originally written in Greek (as a foreign language), which would account
for the syntactic and semantic choices that appear to be of a Semitic origin. It is
clear to him that 'when a text is written in a foreign language the effect of the
mother tongue is no less than when it is subsequently translated' (H. Y. Priebatsch,
'Das Buch Judith und seine hellenistischen Quellen', *ZDPV* 90 [1974], pp. 50-60
[52]).

Septuagint which illustrates one of the most important theological statements in the entire book. It occurs in Jdt. 16.2 (cf. also Jdt. 9.7), in which the narrator says that YHWH puts an end to wars, which is a direct quotation from Exod. 15.3 LXX: θεὸς συντρίβων πολέμους κύριος. The Hebrew text says, in Exod. 15.3, that YHWH is a man of war, not that he puts an end to them. The thesis that the book of Judith, as we have it in Greek, has the status of an original suggests that the text makes/made references to Greek pre-texts.

3. *Judith's Hymn of Praise and the Song of Deborah (Judges 5.2-31 LXX)*

Even a cursory reading of Judith 16 suggests a strong connection between the latter text and the song sung by Deborah and Barak in Judges 5, where Jael is praised for killing Sisera, a commander who had been preparing to attack the people of Israel. As Judith and Jael both use the same method to kill the enemy commander, the similarities between them are striking: 'After the men are asleep, the women murder them by attacking their heads'.[30] The large amount of common ground shared by these two narratives suggests the existence of strong intertextuality between the songs in Judges 5 and Judith 16. Many interpreters have concluded that Judith 16 has more of a connection to Judges 5 than to Exodus 15.[31]

The structures of the two hymns can be, to some extent, compared.[32] Whereas in Jdt. 16.1-17 Judith and the people of Israel sing an antiphonal song, in Judges the two parts are taken alternately by Deborah and Barak. Due to the fact that each singer takes a turn, both Judith and Deborah are referred to in the third person in some verses of the songs, although in other passages they also speak about themselves in the first person.

Gardner has made some perceptive remarks about the structure of the two songs. She divides both the songs of Deborah and Judith into four main sections each:[33]

A	Hymnic Introduction	Judg. 5.2-3	Jdt. 16.1-2
B	Praise of God as Lord over Nature	Judg. 5.4-5	Jdt. 16.13-15b
C	Narration of Epic Event	Judg. 5.6-30	Jdt. 16.3-12
D	Plea to God for Continual Justice	Judg. 5.31	Jdt. 16.15c-17

---

30. White, 'Judith as Heroine', p. 9.
31. Cf. Gardner, 'Song of Praise', p. 422, White, 'Judith as Heroine', p. 11.
32. Cf. Dancy, *Shorter Books*, p. 124; White, 'Judith as Heroine', p. 11.
33. Cf. Gardner, 'Song of Praise', pp. 419-20.

Here Gardner finds a remarkable 'correspondence in literary structure'[34] between the songs of Deborah and Judith, with the only difference lying in the fact that in the song of Judith, the section in which
God is praised as ruler over nature follows the narration of the epic
events, whereas in Judg. 5.2-31 it precedes it.

Both songs summarize the decline of the enemy following Judith's/
Jael's deed. In Jdt. 16.12 the identity of the choice of words[35] suggests
a possible allusion to Judg. 5.31. Whereas these events are sum-
marized in Deborah's song at the end of the song, the song of Judith
summarizes these events much earlier (16.12). In Judith's song the
summary is followed by a new hymnic introduction, in which YHWH
is praised as the Lord of creation.

The structure of Judges 5 proposed by Gardner must be criticized,
because the narrated events that she groups in one section (5.6-30) do
not in fact form a coherent whole, which suggests that this section
needs to have a different kind of structure ascribed to it. With its imperative command to praise God, 5.9-11 should be considered the
beginning of a new section. This is such a marked structuring feature
that 5.6-30 cannot then be considered a unified section. Judges 5.6-8
recall the adversity Israel had faced. The narration of the epic events,
the victory of the people Israel and their God over its enemies, is
limited to 5.12-30.[36]

There are certain differences between the song of Deborah and the
hymn of Judith in terms of main focus and narrative perspective. The
opening passage of Judith 16 focuses on the enemies, but the corre-
sponding section of Judges 5 is concerned exclusively with the travails
of the people of Israel. Judges 5.6-8 mainly describes the chaotic situation in *Israel* when Deborah was still not a Judge, without relating
this in any way to the impending attack by the enemies of the Israelites. The narrative perspective in Jdt. 16.3-4, however, describes
the threat posed by the enemy, as well as the *enemy* itself.

Another decisive difference between the two texts is the order of
occurrence of the passages describing the women's epic deeds. Whereas Judith's occurs at the beginning of the hymn and is followed by the
defeat of Israel's enemies, Jael's comes at the end of the battle. The
reaction of the enemies to Jael's and Judith's deeds also differs in both

34. Gardner, 'Song of Praise', p. 420.

35. ἀπώλοντο ἐκ παρατάξεως κυρίου θεοῦ μου (Jdt. 16.12); οὕτως ἀπόλοιντο
πάντες οἱ ἐχθροί σου, Κύριε (Judg. 5.31).

36. Cf. C. Westermann, *Das Loben Gottes in der Psalmen* (Göttingen: Vandenhoeck & Ruprecht, 1954), pp. 63-64.

songs. Whereas the hymn of Judith describes, in the style of Exodus 15, that the enemies are rigid with fear, the song of Deborah tells of the mother of Sisera waiting for her son, recently fallen in battle, to return.

Only little evidence to support Gardner's thesis 'that he (the author) used the song of Deborah as his literary model'[37] can be found, although Jdt. 16.1-17 does borrow *certain* elements from Deborah's song, such as the change from first to third person narration. In fact the song of Deborah becomes, in certain passages, a kind of structural matrix which, referring to the criterion of 'structurality', indicates a high level of intertextuality.

Indisputably, the most striking parallel between the two songs is that they both sing the praises of one woman's victory over a powerful commander. Both women have played an important role in averting the threat of war against the Israelites, and both songs describe the careful preparations the women make prior to committing their murders. Jael brings the commander (who has asked for water) milk, in fact brings him cream in a splendid bowl (Judg. 5.25). Judith adorns herself resplendently, dazzles Holofernes' eyes, and captivates him with her beauty (Jdt. 16.9). It is worth noting that the songs differ in their descriptions of their respective murders: here the choice of words in Judith 16 does not resemble that of the song of Deborah. In Judith the commander's neck (τράξηλον, 16.9c) is mentioned but not his head, as in Deborah's song (κεφαλὴν, 5.26d).[38]

In addition, dramatic action is not given equal weight in the two songs. In Judith, the murder is described in a single sentence ('and the sword slashed through his neck', 16.9c) that leaves some doubt as to whether or not Judith has actually done the killing. Jael's act of murder is, however, described in far greater detail (5.26c-e). In a four-part verse, the fact that Sisera collapses and dies at Jael's feet is emphasized through repetition. The hymn in the book of Judith lacks graphic descriptions of this kind and tends to avoid both narrative commentary and stylistic flourishes when describing this scene, to the point of not making Judith the focus in describing the murder she committed. Thus, Jdt. 16.1-17 appears to be trying to keep the murder scene out of the foreground of the action. Deborah's song recapitulates the events as they are described in the book of Judges. The song

---

37. Gardner, 'Song of Praise', p. 422.

38. This despite the fact that during the murder scene in the Judith narrative the head (κεφαλή) of Holofernes is itself a key element (see Jdt. 13.6, 7, 8, 9).

of Judith, on the other hand, tries to brighten up both the solemnity of the almost liturgical ceremonial procession, as well as the image of its female protagonist, by omitting any mention of the fact that Judith is the murderer of Holofernes. Instead, the commander's fatal end is depicted as being the result of his own over-indulgence in both war and women: 'Her sandal ravished his eyes; her beauty captivated his mind. And the sword slashed through his neck' (Jdt. 16.9). Judith 16 does not want to make this similarity a central theme, choosing instead to cloak it in an erotically charged description of the murder scene. It is difficult to overlook the referential character of Judith 16 to Judges 5; but what is particularly striking is the dialogical intertextuality in this passage. Judith 16 takes over from Judges 5 the description of the murder of the enemy commander, but nonetheless keeps a discreet distance: about the murder itself, Jdt. 16.1-17 does not choose to report.

The 'hand of a female' (χειρὶ θηλείας) motif plays a central role in the song of Judith: 'The Omnipotent Lord has foiled them by the hand of a female' (Jdt. 16.5). Many exegetes have stated that this motif constitutes a reference to Jael, despite the fact that the expression does not even appear in the song of Deborah. Judges 5 either refers to δεξιαν (right hand) or to χεῖρα ἀπριστεράν (left hand).[39] By saying that 'the Lord will sell Sisera into the hand of a woman' (ἐν χειρὶ γυναικός), Judg. 4.9 makes much clearer than does the song of Deborah the link between the hand and the woman. Inasmuch as (with the sole exception of the genitive object) the motif is semantically identical to the one in Jdt. 16.5 (ἐν χειρὶ θηλείας), the relationship to the narrative (Judg. 4) is therefore made especially clear in this expression. In view of the fact that Judith 16 does not use the word γυνή that is especially linked with Jael, but instead θῆλυς,[40] no direct quote is made, but a striking referentiality can still be said to exist.

It can be no mere coincidence that identical expressions are used. Both texts praise God as the Lord of creation, in which he reveals his greatness. The image 'the mountains shook before the Lord' (Judg. 5.5)[41] is taken up in the song of Judith and changed to: 'For the

---

39. See Judg. 5.26.

40. θῆλυς carries no negative connotation. The word is used primarily in passages in which sexual difference is stressed. For example, it is used when God is described as having created humankind as both male and female (see Gen. 1.27 and Gen. 5.2).

41. ὄρη ἐσαλεύθησαν ἀπὸ προσώπου Κυρίου, Ἐλωεί (Judg. 5.5).

mountains will be moved from their foundations with water, the rocks will melt before you like wax'[42] (Jdt. 16.15).

Another parallelism is that at the end of both songs the events are reflected upon in a *do ut des* schema.[43] The song of Deborah ends, 'So perish all thine enemies, O Lord, but let them who love him be like the sun rising in his might' (Judg. 5.31). The last line of Jdt. 16.17 is a woe against the peoples who have risen up against God's chosen people and who, in so doing, have incurred the wrath of God. But at the same time the Godfearing people are assured that God will shine his mercy upon them (Jdt. 16.15c), and that they are 'great in all things' (Jdt. 16.16c). In conclusion both texts interpret the narrative as a paradigm for Israel's trust in God: a God who intervenes at crucial moments in history, whose reliability is certain, and who treats the just and unjust according to their deeds. At this point the song of Judith picks up a pregnant structure: a confrontation between the Godfearing people and the enemies of Israel.

The semantic relationships between the songs of Deborah and Judith are reflected in the song of Judith's echoing of motifs from Deborah, such as the description of God's power within creation and nature, as well as in the usage of the *do ut des* schema. However, these motifs from the pre-text are used somewhat selectively, and are played upon in such a way that the relationships are not immediately detectable. Yet Jdt. 16.1-17 only indirectly refers to the pre-text, choosing instead to veil the references in its reformulations. In short, it can be said that intertextual relationships between the song of Deborah and Jdt. 16.1-17 do exist, but that they are for the most part occasional allusions. Nevertheless, the intertextual relationships of our text in the book of Judith to the song of Deborah and the narrative in the book of Judges clearly demonstrate that the figure of Jael is a model for that of Judith.[44]

The song of Deborah (Judg. 5.2-31) represents the custom whereby, at the end of a war, women would sing a song of victory.[45] The existence of this practice indicates that women were active participants in the public life of biblical Israel—whether exemplified by Deborah serving as judge or by Jael eliminating the threat to Israel posed by a

---

42. ὄρη γὰρ εκ θεμελίων σὺν ὕδασιν σαλευθήσεται, πέτραι δὲ ἀπὸ προσώπου σου ὡς κηρὸς τακήσονται (Jdt. 16.15).

43. Cf. Gardner, 'Song of Praise', p. 420.

44. The claim that Judith is 'none other than Jael' (E.J. Burns, 'Judith or Jael?', *CBQ* 16 [1955], pp. 12-14 [12], see also E.J. Burns, 'The Genealogy of Judith', *CBQ* 18 [1956], pp. 19-22 [19]), ignores the difference between the two female figures.

45. Cf. Van Dijk-Hemmes, 'Traces of Women's Texts', pp. 43-44.

hostile commander. With the intertextual relationships to the song of Deborah the song of Judith joins the tradition of women singing victory songs. But at the same time this text goes a step beyond the mere endorsement of an already existing tradition.

4. *Judith's Hymn of Praise and the Song of the Sea (Exodus 15.1-18 LXX)*

Like the womens' song of victory, the song of Moses celebrates the defeat of the enemy and the greatness of YHWH. However, in doing so, this song also usurps the position that customarily belonged to a woman, namely Miriam. It displaces the tradition of women singing victory songs.[46] The words of the song, instead of being sung by a woman, are now sung by Moses. In the following the fact that the song sung by Moses after Israel's passage through the Red Sea strongly influenced Jdt. 16.1-17 is to be shown. 'As Moses sang a song of triumph after the deliverance from Egypt, so Judith...sings the song of her victory, giving praise to God "great and glorious, wonderful in strength, invincible"' (16.13).[47]

Like Judges 5 and Judith 16 this song is an antiphonal (see Exod. 15.1), but here the parts are taken by Moses and the sons of Israel, which means that the text is lacking the female voice that creates the relationship between the songs of Deborah and Judith. In her structural comparison of the songs of Moses and Judith, Gardner hardly found any parallels between them.[48] However, the following comparative analysis reveals that whole passages in the song of Judith are based on the song of Moses. According to Moore[49] three elements in particular show striking similarities:

Hymnic introduction: God makes an end to wars	Jdt. 16.1-2	Exod. 15.1-3
Description of the enemy and his plans	Jdt. 16.3-4	Exod. 15.9
Reaction to God's intervention	Jdt. 16.10-12	Exod. 15.14-16

The first clear references to Exodus 15 in Judith 16 come in the hymnic introduction, which invites to praise God as he makes an end to wars. At some points, the same structure and choice of synonymous words are to be found: whereas Exod. 15.1b begins by a self-request,

---

46. Cf. Van Dijk-Hemmes, 'Traces of Women's Texts', p. 40.

47. E.M. Schuller, 'The Apocrypha', in C.A. Newsom and S.H. Ringe (eds.), *The Women's Bible Commentary* (London: SPCK, 1992), pp. 235-43 (242).

48. Cf. Gardner, 'Song of Praise', p. 418. She bases her analysis on the Hebrew, not on the Greek version of the Exodus text, and therefore overlooks both structural and contextual parallelisms.

49. Cf. Moore, *Judith*, p. 256.

ἄισωμεν τῷ κυρίῳ, in the subjunctive plural, Jdt. 16.1d contains the same structure and expressions, but formulates the latter in the imperative: ἄσατε τῷ κυρίῳ.

At another point, the hymn of Judith echoes and uses structures from the song in Exodus 15. In both songs, the enemy introduces a description of his plans with the word εἶπεν. Whereas in Exod. 15.9 the enemy uses direct speech, Assur's plan is recounted in indirect speech in Jdt. 16.4. It is more than striking that both texts use five verbs in describing the enemy's plans. The fact that, moreover, the same or synonymous vocabulary is used, is further proof of the high level of intertextuality between the two texts. In Jdt. 16.4 Assur says that he would slay the young men by the sword (ἀνελεῖν ἐν ῥομφαίᾳ) and abduct the women for cheap spoil: (σκυλεῦσεαι). And in his speech in Exod. 15.9 the enemy (Pharaoh) says that he will slay the Israelites by the sword (ἀνελῶ τῇν μαχαίρᾳ μου) and will divide the spoil (μεριῶ σκῦλα).

A third analogy is that in the two songs the reactions of the enemies and nations[50] to the changes wrought by Judith's or God's actions are described as reactions of fear and horror. Synonyms are used to describe the reactions of the enemy and the people to God's acts: in Exod. 15.14-16, 'are troubled', 'pangs take hold', 'dread and horror',[51] and 'petrified' parallel 'shuddered', 'were daunted', 'cowered in fear', 'screamed' and 'ran' in Jdt. 16.10-11. In addition, a universalizing tendency in the description of the enemy is perceptible: Exodus 15 makes God's triumph over Pharaoh more glorious, listing as it does which peoples should tremble before YHWH: the Philistines, the Edomites, the Moabites and the Canaanites. The same occurs in the hymn of Judith: not only Assur,[52] the aggressor in Jdt. 16.3, but even the Persians and Medes tremble with fear in 16.10.

Thus the preceding analysis has shown that Exodus 15 is not only a reference for the hymn in the book of Judith, but also that Craven's

---

50. Both the hymn of Judith and the song of Moses refer to the enemy as a pursuer. See Exod. 15.9 (διώξας) and Jdt. 16.2 (ἐκ χειρὸς καταδιωκόντων).

51. The connection between φόβος and τρόμος that is made in Exod. 15 is not found in the hymn itself, but is not unknown in the book of Judith, as Jdt. 2.28 appropriates this expression in describing the reaction to the annihilation of the Assyrian army: καὶ ἐπέπεσεν φόβος καὶ τρόνος. The same is true of Jdt. 15.2, where the people who once made the whole earth tremble with terror now experience the same fear themselves: καὶ ἐπέπεσεν ἐπʼ αὐτοὺς τρόνος καὶ φόβος.

52. Here, the fictitious character of the book of Judith is once again clearly in evidence: Nebuchadnezzar (in reality) was the king of Babylon, not Assur (cf. van Henten, 'Alternative Leader', p. 226).

observation, that both songs are 'remarkably similar in terms of function, form, and content'[53] cannot be gainsaid. It can be said that several passages in Exodus 15 served as a linguistic and structural model for Judith 16, and that the structural homologies are more distinctive than in the song of Deborah. At least the passages in the song of Moses in which the enemy first describes his plans and after which the reaction of the enemy and the people of Israel is described, appear to have served as a structural model for Judith 16. Thus, a high level of intertextual reference within the framework of the criterion of 'structurality' can be said to exist in these texts.

What the two texts have most strikingly in common are the quotations. Judith 16 contains two direct quotations from Exodus 15. When Jdt. 16.2 says, 'For the Lord is a God who crushes wars'[54] it is clearly quoting Exod. 15.3, which says: 'The Lord crushes wars, Lord is his name'.[55] Shekan finds this quotation problematic as he hypothesizes that Exodus 15 'is the poetic prototype for the canticle of Jdt'.[56] Because he believes that Judith 16 used the Hebrew text as a model, he is unable to account for the fact that the Greek text is quoted at this point.[57] Thus the song of Judith joins the theological tradition of the Septuagint. YHWH is not a man of war, instead he crushes wars, as the song in the Greek version of Exodus states. In this quotation, a significant textual element is echoed, because here Judith 16 refers explicitly, rather than just alluding to, the Exodus tradition. Is the quotation as such recognizable? Inasmuch as Jdt. 16.2 uses the quotation in the same context, namely, the hymnic introduction, as the book of Exodus uses it and the quotation also echoes one of the most programmatic theological statements in the Greek version of the Exodus narrative, the evidence in support of a high degree of referentiality and selectivity is here extremely persuasive. It can be said that Exod. 15.1-18 becomes the semantic setting for the entire hymn of Judith. 'The trenchantly selected detail calls up the entire context from which it originates; the brief quote translates the whole pre-text into a new realm of meaning'.[58] As a synecdoche this quotation calls to mind the entire Exodus tradition, which is for Israel not only a historical event

53. T. Craven, *Artistry and Faith in the Book of Judith* (SBLDS, 7; Chico, CA: Scholars Press, 1983), p. 111.
54. ὅτι θεὸς συντρίβων πολέμους κύριος.
55. κύριος συντρίβων πολέμους, κύριος ὄνομα αὐτῷ.
56   Shekan, 'Hand of Judith', p. 96.
57. Cf. Shekan, 'Hand of Judith', p. 104.
58. Pfister, 'Intertextualität', p. 29.

but also an *Erinnerungsfigur*.[59] A further criterion satisfied by the text
for a high level of intertextuality is communicativity, because the
recipients are meant both to recognize the quotation and with it the
intertextual relationship to the song, and to interpret their liberation
through Judith's actions as a new experience of the Exodus. In the
new historical situation, God reveals himself to be a God of Exodus
who leads the people of Israel out of oppression and bondage.

In the section in which the theology of creation is developed, Judith
16 also borrows an entire sentence, ἀπέστειλας τὸ πνεῦμά σου, from
Exod. 15.10, placing it in a new semantic context. This shows that the
second part of the song of Judith also refers to the song of Moses.[60]
Whereas in Exodus the sending forth of the spirit is related to the
statement that the Red Sea covered the enemy, in Judith this action on
God's part is related to the theology of creation. God sends his spirit
forth and makes all creation (Jdt. 16.14). Exodus 15.8 neither portrays
God's actions against the background of creation nor portrays God as
creator as such. Instead, YHWH is the one who can part the waters
(ὕδωρ) with his breath (πνεύματος) so that the sea stands like a wall.
Moreover, he makes the waters recede and the enemy sink like lead
into the turbulent waters (ἐν ὕδατι). In Jdt. 16.15a God's power also
lies in the fact that he can move the mountains and the sea. However,
the new semantic field makes the second quotation less recognizable
than the first. Its referential character is not as evident as in the relationship between Jdt. 16.2 and Exod. 15.3.

The songs in Judith 16 and Exodus 15 praise YHWH's greatness,
which is manifested by his liberation of Israel. The glorifying of God
in Judith 16 demonstrates a strong affinity to the language that is used
to praise God in his greatness in the song of Moses.[61]

The 'theology of Zion'[62] found in the Exodus hymn is indirectly
referred to in the hymn of Judith, when Jdt. 16.2b says that God has
torn Judith out of the hands of her pursuers and delivered her into the

---

59. J. Assmann, *Das kulturelle Gedächtnis: Schrift, Erinnerung und politische Identität in frühen Hochkulturen* (Munich: Beck, 1992), p. 201.

60. It is not only the 'canticle in Jdt. 16.1-12 [that] is the new Song of the Sea in Exod. 15.1-18' (J.F. Cragham, 'Esther, Judith, and Ruth: Paradigms of Human Liberation', *BTB* 1 [1982], pp. 11-19 [12]), there are references to Exod. 15.1-18 throughout the entire song of Judith.

61. μεγέθει βραχίονός σου (Exod. 15.16)   κύριε, μέγας εἶ (Jdt. 16.13a).
    δεδόξασται ἐν ἰσχύι (Exod. 15.6)   καὶ ἔνδοξος (Jdt. 16.13b).
    θαυμαστὸς ἐν δόξαις (Exod. 15.11)   θαυμαστὸς ἐν ἰσχύι (Jdt. 16.13b).

62. E. Zenger, *Das Buch Exodus* (Düsseldorf: Patmos, 1978), p. 151.

camp of his people (εἰς παρεμβολὰς αὐτοῦ ἐν μέσῳ λαοῦ). This expression recalls the years of wandering through the desert from the book of Exodus, when God accompanied the Israelites' encampment and lived in the holy tent.[63] In the book of Judith, this encampment now is the temple on Mt Zion, the place where the ark of the covenant 'as a sign of God's presence'[64] is. Exodus 15.17 says that God calls his people to his holy city. YHWH leads them up to the 'mount of his heritage', in other words, Zion. The song of Moses does not make any mention of the Israelites' *acquisition of land*; the Exodus from Egypt leads directly to *Zion*.[65] Similarly, as God leads his people Israel out of Egypt to the temple, this event is repeated through Judith when, as the hymn is being sung, she leads the people in the procession to Jerusalem. The liberation in Exodus, as well as the liberation that God achieves with Judith's 'help', leads to the permanent presence of God in the temple on Mt Zion.[66] That the two texts have many points in common in terms of their content indicates a high degree of referentiality between them.

The motif of the hand of God plays a significant role in Exodus 15.[67] In this respect, the expressions ἡ δεξιά σου (15.6a) and ἡ δεξιά σου χεὶρ (15.6b) are used. Judith 16 echoes the hand motif, but here it becomes a woman's hand (Jdt. 16.6). As the hand of God saves the Israelites from Pharaoh in Exodus, so God saves Israel once again, this time from the despot Nebuchadnezzar and by the hand of Judith:[68] 'The Lord Almighty has foiled them by the hand of a female' (Jdt 16.6). Moreover, the theme of outwitting and tempting the enemy is no stranger to the book of Exodus.[69] Gardner sees the 'hand' motif as being a key element, which distinguishes the two hymns. 'In Exodus

---

63. Cf. E. Haag, *Studien zum Buche Judith: Seine theologische Bedeutung und literarische Eigenart* (Trierer theologische Studien, 16; Trier: Paulinus, 1963), p. 56.

64. Haag, *Studien*, p. 56.

65. Cf. H. Spiekermann, *Heilsgegenwart: Eine Theologie der Psalmen* (FRLANT, 148; Göttingen: Vandenhoek & Ruprecht, 1989), p. 108.

66. It is true of the Judith narrative as a whole that Judith saves the temple in Jerusalem from being destroyed and profaned once again (see Jdt. 4.1-3) (cf. L.B. Elder, 'Judith', in E. Schüssler Fiorenza [ed.], *Searching the Scriptures*. II. *A Feminist Commentary* [London: SCM Press, 1995], pp. 455-69 [467]).

67. Cf. Shekan, 'Hand of Judith', pp. 96-108.

68. Cf. Shekan, 'Hand of Judith', p. 103.

69. Haag has demonstrated that the passage in Exod. 14.1-4, which says that YHWH caused Pharaoh to be hard-hearted, has a similar structure: 'YHWH tempts Pharao because the helplessness and despair of the Israelites seem to the crafty Pharao to create a good opportunity to attack them and to place them again under Egypt's yoke' (Haag, *Studien*, p. 104). He is of the opinion, 'that the enemy due to

God alone makes an appearance in the war scenes whereas in Judith his instruments (Judith and then the people) are the ones who overcome the enemy, although they recognize that He granted them victory.'[70] Not only has the hand been viewed as 'a female instrument of the male deity'[71] and the song interpreted as saying that Judith praises only God for bringing victory;[72] but it has also been stated by some that God uses the hand of a female because this adds 'to the disgrace of the defeated foe'[73] and that the hymn uses the expression 'hand of a female' in order to stress this. Interpretations of this passage are more androcentric than the text itself.

This motif must rather be interpreted differently: YHWH intervenes in history by Judith's hand. This phenomenon is a common characteristic of Jewish narratives in the Hellenistic period, in which a direct intervention by God was no longer believable; such intervention could only come about through the agency of human beings. In the entire book of Judith, only once is YHWH described as the subject of an action[74]—an act of listening to the pleas of his people for liberation;[75] the liberation itself does not become reality through him alone but through Judith's hand. Therefore even this action is not an immediate one. Here the hand of Judith is a synecdoche for her whole person. Thus she is an epiphany of God.[76] Judith is an embodiment of God in a new Exodus.

That the hymn of Judith has a strong intertextual relationship with Exod. 15.1-18 is indicated by the density of references; the quantity of references contributes to this strong intertextuality as well as the quality. The view that Jdt. 16.1-17 'was inspired by the victory song in Exod.15'[77] is proven by the intertextual relationships, which are as well an indication that the book of Judith was attempting to represent

its own over-indulgence loses sight of YHWH's true greatness, and at long last, blinded by its own fault, brings ruin upon itself' (104).

70. Gardner, 'Song of Praise', p. 419; see also Craven, *Artistry and Faith*, p. 91.

71. P.J. Milne, 'What Shall We Do with Judith? A Feminist Reassessment of a Biblical "Heroine"', *Semeia* 62 (1993), pp. 37-58 (55).

72. Cf. Milne, 'Judith', p. 51. She states that the role of hero is assigned to God and not to Judith due to the fact that Judith's victory is attributed only to God.

73. Enslin, *Book of Judith*, p. 125 n. 10.

74. Against this background, Milne's suggestion that God be assigned the role of hero in the Judith narrative seems debatable (cf. Milne, 'Judith', p. 51).

75. See Jdt. 4.13.

76. Cf. Zenger, 'Wir erkennen', pp. 31-32.

77. E. Zenger, 'Der Judithroman als Traditionsmodell des Jahweglaubens', *TTZ* 83 (1974), pp. 65-80 (72).

the theological structure of the events in Exodus.[78] The theology of the hymn thus becomes the theology of the Exodus. The God of Israel is remembered as the one who refuses war and oppression, the one who sides with the weak and oppressed (see Jdt. 16.11) in their struggle for liberation and freedom.

5. *Judith and her Models*

Notwithstanding the existence of some disagreement as to whether Exod. 15.1-18 is a post-exilic text that was added to Exodus 14[79] or whether the song Miriam sings might be concealed beneath the textual surface of Exod. 15.1-18 and that the text might have been attributed to Moses in a later version,[80] the structure of the end text nonetheless presents clear evidence of fragmentation arising from revised editing. The narrative context of Exodus 15 offers two different endings for the narrative. In the context of the end text, the hymn sung by Miriam and the women after the passage through the Red Sea (Exod. 15.20-21) is only to be taken as a response to the song of Moses (Exod. 15.1-18), 'an afterthought, a token of the female presence'.[81] 'That the song of Moses, a premature answer to its successor, is positioned before Miriam's song can and must almost certainly be explained by androcentric motives'.[82] Rewriting by later editors deprived Miriam of her role as singer, thus relegating to the background her position as a leading character who stands beside Moses during the events recounted in Exodus.

Through its references to Exod. 15.1-18, the hymn of the book of Judith is a narrative re-invention of the Exodus. The related literary process, whereby the hymn of Judith comments upon its own pre-text

78. Cf. Schüssler Fiorenza, *In Memory of Her: A Feminist Theological Reconstruction of Christian Origins* (New York: Crossroad, 1983), p. 115.

79. See H.-P. Mathys, who reads Exod. 15.1-18 as a post-exilic insertion that attempts to reappraise the lack of continuity of YHWH's actions, a subject that preoccupied the Israelites since the Babylonian exile. For him the text does so by placing more emphasis on YHWH's continuous redeeming presence in the temple and his majestic power, than on single contingent interventions by God (cf. Mathys, *Dichter und Beter*, p. 175).

80. Cf. A. Brenner, *The Israelite Woman: Social Role and Literary Type in Biblical Narrative* (The Biblical Seminar, 2; Sheffield: JSOT Press, 1985), p. 52.

81. P. Trible, 'Bringing Miriam out of the Shadows', in A. Brenner (ed.), *A Feminist Companion to Exodus to Deuteronomy* (The Feminist Companion to the Bible, 6; Sheffield: Sheffield Academic Press, 1994), pp. 166-68 (171).

82. Van Dijk-Hemmes, 'Traces of Women's Texts', p. 40.

and lays the groundwork for a new situation, demonstrates the high dialogical quality of its intertextual references. 'The tradition is modified and re-narrated.'[83] The fact that a woman, Judith, now sings in praise of a new Exodus restores to Miriam the voice she has lost in the book of Exodus. Such a relecture derives support from the way in which the embedding of the song of Judith within the narrative refers to Exod. 15.20-21: 'All women of Israel flocked to see her and sang her praise; some performed a dance in her honor' (Jdt. 15.12). Like Miriam, who leads the festive procession of the women (Exod. 15.20), Judith also places herself at the head of the procession, to lead the women to Jerusalem (Jdt. 15.13). The fact that the song, in which Moses (according the book of Exodus) praises the greatness of God for leading the Israelites out of exile in Egypt is now restored to the women's tradition, as the women now sing in praise of YHWH's greatness, represents the literary restoration of Miriam's voice. Thus this passage satisfies, at least in part, the criteria for an 'F voice', insofar as the text contains traces of a less androcentric intent.[84] The androcentric frame within which Miriam was almost completely silenced cannot be applied to the book of Judith in this passage. Thus is Miriam's voice, taken from her by the revised version of androcentric editors, restored.

Can the hymn of Judith also be said to be a narrative re-reading of the song of Deborah? In the song of Judith, the theme that women play a significant role in saving Israel from its enemies is taken from the song of Deborah: Jael and Judith defeat the enemy commander. But YHWH plays a less central role in Judges 5[85] than in the book of Judith, which nonetheless does not mean that the text minimizes the role of women in the liberation of Israel. The hand of Jael is not explicitly connected to YHWH's actions. YHWH delivers Sisera into the hands of Jael; but Judith's hand is the one by which God intervenes in history. Judith is God's epiphany. The song of Deborah describes an epiphany as well, but in this instance YHWH uses cosmic means to achieve his ends.[86] According to Jdt. 16.6 God outwits Israel's enemies by the hand of Judith, who thus becomes a 'female epiphany'.[87]

---

83. K. Butting, *Die Buchstaben werden sich noch wundern: Innerbiblische Kritik als Wegweisung feministischer Hermeneutik* (Berlin: Alektor, 1993), p. 171.

84. Cf. Van Dijk-Hemmes, 'Traces of Women's Texts', p. 106.

85. Cf. A. van der Kooij, 'On Male and Female Views in Judges 4 and 5', in B. Becking and M. Dijkstra (eds.), *On Reading Prophetic Texts: Gender-specific and Related Studies in Memory of Fokkelien van Dijk-Hemmes* (Biblical Interpretation Series, 18; Leiden: E.J. Brill, 1996), pp. 135-52 (149).

86. See the song of Deborah, esp. Judg. 5.13, 20.

87. Zenger, 'Wir erkennen', p. 31. This is not at all to suggest that Judith is

YHWH intervenes only through Judith. Thus, with the help of the referentiality of Jael and Judith, actions taken by women for the benefit of Israel are combined with YHWH's actions on behalf of his people.

The motif of the hand also reveals a key difference between Exod. 15.1-18 and Judith 16, because in Exodus 15 it is not the human (Moses') hand, but in this case the divine hand that is acting. YHWH parts the waters alone, and it is the action of his hand that is praised in song.[88] Moses does not play an important role in Exod. 15.1-18: he is merely the singer of the song. Thus, the question arises as to whether any relationship between Judith and Moses can be established.

By the mere fact that Judith gives voice to a new song of Exodus, the relationship to Moses can be said to exist. The song of Judith interprets the events that the book of Judith reports on as a new Exodus. In this sense, Judith also becomes an agent of actualization for the figure of Moses in a new literary context, in a new narrative of the Exodus. By consulting the Exodus narrative it becomes evident that the figure of Judith is given some of Moses' attributes. In the portion of the narrative concerning the rescue at the Red Sea, YHWH also uses the hand of Moses to part the waters and to make the sea recede, which prevents the Egyptians from attacking the Israelites.[89] Thus does YHWH act through Moses' hand in Exodus. That a woman modeled on Jael is here associated with the events recounted in Exodus (in which Moses is the central figure) appropriates for women one of the most significant biblical traditions, the Exodus tradition. Against the background of the song of Judith, the Exodus is one in which women play an important role, not only because they sing the praises of the events therein recounted, but also because they take an active part: a woman becomes the savior of the people of Israel.[90] In a situation fraught with danger, Judith becomes an alternative leader.[91] Moreover, like Moses (with the song of Moses as background), she leads

---

inviolable. To stress that a role is attributed to the figure of Judith that renders her 'superior to all male acts' (Van Henten, 'Alternative Leader', p. 246) runs the risk of creating a structure that loses sight of the threat of rape by Holofernes. (See Jdt. 12.16: When Judith entered and lay down, Holofernes was beside himself with desire, and his brain was reeling; and he was very eager to have relations with her. From the day he had first seen her he had been watching for an opportunity to seduce her.)

88. See Exod. 15.12.
89. See Exod. 14.15, 21, 26, 27.
90. Cf. van Henten, 'Alternative Leader', p. 251.
91. Cf. van Henten, 'Alternative Leader', pp. 238-45, esp. 243-44. He points out

the Israelites to Jerusalem, to Zion.[92] In this respect, Judith acquires attributes that actualize the figure of Moses: she becomes the leader of a new Exodus from Egypt. But she does not take over *every* aspect of this role. The presence of so many parallelisms should not obscure the fact that Judith's appearance in the narrative as a female Moses can only be an episode; for, at the very moment in which the threat to Israel is removed, the text sends her back to her private sphere of widowhood,[93] thereby re-establishing the androcentric frame of the narrative. Moses will accompany the people of Israel long after the events at the Red Sea, whereas Judith has to make her exit, so as to allow for the reestablishment of previous relationships and the return of male leaders.[94]

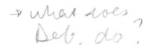

that the role of Judith as alternative leader in a 'socio-historical context' takes a Hasmonaean critical stance, qualifying 1 Macc. in particular.

92. Whereas Moses will not reach Zion, Judith will still have the opportunity to pray to YHWH in Jerusalem.

93. A.-J. Levine, 'Sacrifice and Salvation: Otherness and Domestication in the Book of Judith', in J.C. VanderKam (ed.), *'No One Spoke Ill of Her': Essays on Judith* (SBL Early Judaism and its Literature, 2; Atlanta: 1992), pp. 17-30 (17); reprinted in A. Brenner (ed.), *A Feminist Companion to Esther, Judith and Susanna* (The Feminist Companion to the Bible, 7; Sheffield: Sheffield Academic Press, 1995), pp. 209-223.

94. A woman, whose beauty gives her such great power that she can bring about a man's death (even if it is the enemy commander), should not have unlimited use of this power. She must be made to return to the traditional role of women in her society so that she does not threaten continuance of the patriarchal hierarchy.

THE STORY OF JEPHTHAH'S DAUGHTER IN THE MIDRASH

Shulamit Valler

The double tragedy in the biblical story of Jephthah and his daughter (Judg. 11.29-40), cannot but impress the reader.

The structure, the protagonists' dialogue, the daughter's companions who form a kind of chorus, and the content, in which a father sacrifices his daughter to satisfy the deity, bring to mind Greek tragedies of the sixth and fifth centuries BCE, like that of Iphigenia, sacrificed by her father Agamemnon to placate the gods. The ideological concept within the Jephthah story also resembles the concept in Greek tragedies: heroes are caught up in crisis and calamity not because they have done wrong, but because it has been decreed by higher powers they can neither control nor understand.

In the biblical story both Jephthah and his daughter are victims of their faith. Jephthah vows to offer up as a burnt offering whatever comes from the doors of his house to meet him when he returns in peace from the war with the Ammonites. He may have been stupid or hasty, but certainly not a cruel father who knowingly planned his daughter's death. In his haste, Jephthah's vow did not properly define how payment was to be made. He did not succeed in formulating his vow to specify that he did not intend to make an actual sacrifice. Like Samson's mother (Judg. 15.5) or Hannah (1 Sam. 1.11-28), he said 'shall be the Lord's', but added 'I will offer it up for a burnt offering'.[1] He may have been affected by a Canaanite custom that did not shrink from human sacrifice, but he cannot possibly have imagined that he was going to sacrifice his only daughter: the exclamation: 'Alas, my daughter! Thou hast brought me very low, and thou art one of them that trouble me', sounds credible indeed. Moreover, the object of the vow, 'whatsoever cometh forth', is in the masculine gender, and this formulation may have been intended to keep his daughter outside the payment of the vow. Perhaps his vow was framed that way because he knew it was a custom for girls to come out to meet returning

---

1.   All biblical passages are from the translation of the KJV.

conquerors (Exod. 15.20-21; 1 Sam. 13.6-7). The narrator's emphasis, 'and she was his only child; beside her he had neither son nor daughter', indicates that he wished to present Jephthah as a hapless individual who fell into his own snare, not a cruel and heartless man. (The Hebrew may hint that this may mean that Jephthah, unlike his wife, had no other children, or, alternatively, that since the daughter was still a virgin he had no grandchildren.)

In the biblical story the daughter too is convinced that her father has to make good his vow. Father and daughter equally dread the idea of breaking a vow. He says, 'I have opened my mouth unto the Lord and I cannot go back', and she says, 'If thou hast opened thy mouth unto the Lord, do unto me according to that which has proceeded out of thy mouth; for as much as the Lord has taken vengeance of thee of thine enemies, even of the children of Ammon'.

Father and daughter, then, are victims of the tragic situation they find themselves in through no fault of their own, for 'the spirit of the Lord' was upon Jephthah when he set out to war, and his vow was a vow to the Lord. Only God could have prevented the tragedy, and He did not keep the daughter either from going out to meet her father or from returning to him later so that he could 'do with her according to his vow'.

Thus far the biblical story. As for the Jewish Sages, they could not accept a God whose deeds are incomprehensible, and in whose hands human beings are mere playthings.

In the Bible itself questions of divine injustice do arise. The biblical response—and one of the answers of Greek philosophy—that divine justice is beyond human understanding could not satisfy the Sages. As true believers, they could not accept the possibility of any fault in the conduct of God, the very embodiment of morality. For that reason, the compilers of the *Aggadah* tried hard to impute wickedness to Jephthah and thus foil any possibility of placing the Holy One, Blessed be He, in any connection with the terrible deed of offering up the daughter as a sacrifice. In their efforts, they wrought a complete transformation in the image of Jephthah. They often did this with biblical figures, using the facts stated in the Bible, without deviation, to create a new character for their own purposes.

The biblical story of Jephthah puts his character through several transformations. In the beginning of the chapter he is a ruffian, with no worthy family connections, who gathers a gang of vain men around him. Later on this muscle man shows himself a shrewd leader, coolly planning his career, thoroughly familiar with his people's history and a great believer in the God of Israel.

True, in his words to the King of Ammon: 'Wilt thou not possess
that which Chemosh thy god giveth thee to possess? So whomsoever
the Lord our God shall drive out from before us, them will we possess' (Judg. 11.24), there is a pagan perception. But this can also be
seen as a diplomatic statement, one in which Jephthah talks to the
Ammonite king in a language that he will understand, which grants
the Israelite judge an additional dimension of intellectual ability.

Jephthah's meeting with his daughter after he returns from the war
is the beginning of his decline. He emerges hurt and insulted when he
encounters an unexpected problem, when the Ephraimites threaten
him: 'We will burn thy house upon thee with fire' (Judg. 12.1).

His first reaction is not violent. He explains why he did not include
them in the fight against Ammon, and expresses wonder at their
vengeful intent. His next reaction, however, is violent indeed. He starts
a bloody civil war, and treats its refugees with cynical cruelty. Finally,
Jephthah again becomes the ruffian he once was. He is no longer
merely a local tough, but a ruffian directing the barbaric murder of
hosts of weak, innocent people.

In the midrash, the later Jephthah takes over completely. In their
attempts to explain the frightful story about the sacrifice of the daughter in a manner that will keep their faith intact, the Sages who ex-
pounded the story deprive the character of Jephthah of the few good
points set forth in the Hebrew Bible. The various midrashim presented here are first of all a series of reprimands to Jephthah. In some,
the reproaches are in ascending order of severity as his deeds become
worse and worse, to the point where there is not even a suspicion that
God had any influence on the events.

There are stories about Jephthah and his daughter in four midrashic
collections, and in Tractate *Ta'anit* of the Babylonian Talmud.[2] Since I
am not concerned here with comparisons or with finding an authentic
version, but rather with the purposes behind the interpretations,
I shall focus the discussion on *Genesis Rabbah*,[3] the oldest of the Amoraic
midrashim, and on the expanded and improved version in the
Tanḥuma,[4] a relatively late collection. My notes cite the differences

---

2.   The texts from tractate Ta'anit have been quoted from the translation of
J. Rabinovitz (ed. I. Epstein; London: Soncino Press, 1938).

3.   The passages from *Gen. R.* have been quoted from the translation of
H. Freedman (ed. H. Freedman; London: Soncino Press, 1961 [1939]).

4.   The passages from Midrash *Tanḥuma Hakadum* have been translated from
the original.

between details in the midrashim in these collections, and those found elsewhere.

Gen. R. 60.3 begins by citing Jephthah's vow. Says Jephthah:

> Whatsoever cometh forth of the doors of my house to meet me when I return in peace from the children of Ammon shall surely be the Lord's, and I will offer it up for a burnt offering.

The midrash links these words to the prayer of Abraham's eldest servant when seeking a bride for his master's son (Gen. 24.12-14). The servant said:

> O Lord God of my master Abraham, I pray thee, send me good speed this day, and shew kindness to my master Abraham. Behold I stand here by the well of water, and the daughters of the men of the city come out to draw water. And let it come to pass that the damsel to whom I shall say, Let down thy pitcher, I pray thee, that I may drink, and she shall say, Drink, and I will give thy camels drink also, let the same be she that thou has appointed for thy servant Isaac; and thereby shall I know that thou has shewed kindness unto my master.

The midrash expounds:

> Four asked improperly: three were granted their request in a fitting manner, and the fourth, in an unfitting manner. They are: Eliezer, Caleb, Saul and Jephthah.[5] Eliezer: *So let it come to pass, that the damsel*—even a bondmaid![6] Yet God prepared Rebekah for him, and granted his request in a fitting manner. Caleb: *He that smiteth Kiriat-sepher, and taketh it, to him will I give Achsah my daughter to wife* (Judg. 1.12)—it might even be a

5. In *Lev. R.* 37.3 the order is different. 'Four people began their supplication by making vows. Three of them made their request in an improper manner and the Holy One, Blessed be He, answered them favourably, while one made the request in an improper manner and the Omnipresent answered him correspondingly. They are as follows: Eliezer the servant of Abraham, Saul, Jephthah and Caleb'.

The order in *Gen. R.* is chronological, except for Jephthah, the exception, and so is more plausible.

In *Ta'an.* 4a the number is different, though the order remains: 'R. Samuel b. Nahmani said in the name of R. Jonathan: Three [men] made haphazard requests, two of them were fortunate in the reply they received and one was not, namely Eliezer the servant of Abraham; Saul, the son of Kish; and Jephthah the Gileadite'. (Possibly there are three in *Ta'anit* because the fourth is Knesset Israel who asked, and God answered her. It is also possible, as Albeck writes in his explanation of *Gen. R.*, that because all were connected with the marriage of a daughter, like the act of Abraham's servant, the *Gen. R.* midrash linked them together.)

6. 'Even a bondmaid!' In *Lev. R.*, 'If a Canaanite slave girl or a harlot had come out, would you still have said, "*Let the same be she that Thou has appointed for Thy servant, even for Isaac?*"' In *Ta'anit*, She might have been lame or blind.

slave![7] But God chose Othniel for him. Saul: *And it shall be, that the man who killeth him, the king will enrich him with great riches, and will give him his daughter* (1 Sam. 17.25)—it might even be slave.[8] But God prepared David for him. Jephthah asked in an unfitting manner, as it says, *And Jephthah vowed a vow unto the Lord, and said, Then it shall be that, whatsoever cometh forth…and it shall be the Lord's, and I will offer it up for a burnt offering* (Judg. 11.30-31). Said the Holy One, Blessed be He, to him: 'Then had a camel or an ass or a dog come forth, thou wouldst have offered it up for a burnt-offering!'[9] What did the Lord do? He answered him unfittingly and prepared his daughter for him, as it says, *And Jephthah came…and behold, his daughter came out to meet him* (Judg. 11.34).

To understand why of all four who asked, or who began their vows improperly, God answered only Jephthah unfittingly, one must consider the style changes in *Genesis Rabbah*. The Sage's reply to Abraham's servant is verbal: 'Even a bondmaid!' By contrast, God's response was an act, not words: 'God prepared Rebekah for him and granted his request in a fitting manner'. The style of the responses to Caleb and Saul is similar. In both cases the Sage's reaction is verbal: 'It might even have been a slave'. God's response, however, is active: in the former, 'God prepared Othniel for him' and in the latter, 'God prepared David for him'.

In Jephthah's case, however, 'He asked in an unfitting manner and God answered him in an unfitting manner', after which there are details about what he asked and what God replied verbally, and only at the end are we told what God did. 'Said the Holy One, Blessed be He: "Then had a camel or an ass or a dog come forth , thou wouldst

7.   'It might have been a slave'. As for Caleb in *Lev. R.*, 'If a Canaanite, or a bastard, or a slave had captured it, would you have given him your daughter?' *Ta'anit* does not mention Caleb.

8.   'It could have been a slave'. About Saul in *Lev. R.*, 'If an Ammonite, or a bastard, or a slave had killed him, would you have given him your daughter?' *Ta'anit*: '[He] might have been a slave or a bastard'.

9.   'If a camel, or an ass, or a dog had come forth, would you have offered it up to me as a burnt-offering?' In *Lev. R.* 'If a camel, or an ass, or a dog had come out, would you have offered it for a burnt-offering?' In *Ta'anit*, 'It might have been an unclean thing'. In *Yalquṭ Shim'oni* for Judges, Sign 25, there is a slightly different version: 'Four asked unfittingly. Three were answered in a fitting manner and one was answered in an unfitting manner. Eliezer said "Let the maiden…" A maid with one hand could have come out or a bondmaid, and he would have married her to…and the Holy One, Blessed be He, prepared Rebekah… Caleb said, "Whoever smites", and it could even have been a slave, would he have given him his daughter? The Holy One Blessed be He prepared Othniel for him. Saul said "The man who"—a black man might have come forth… Would he have given him his daughter? The Holy One Blessed be He prepared David for him.'

have offered it up to me as a burnt offering?"' Only after that comes, 'What did the Lord do? He answered him unfittingly and prepared his daughter for him'. In *Leviticus Rabbah*[10] God answers all the makers of vows, including Jephthah, in the same way. And in the midrash in *Ta'anit*, the anonymous voice answers them all with questions: 'Might it have been even...?' after which the formula is 'He answered him (un)fittingly, he prepared for him...' In these two midrashim there is no difference between the style used with Jephthah and that used with the petitioners who received fitting responses.

If we compare the formulation of responses to Eliezer, to Caleb and to Saul in *Genesis Rabbah* with the formulation of the response to Jephthah, we note a deliberate stylistic deviation, apparently intended to emphasize the difference between his request and the requests of those mentioned before him.

Eliezer, Caleb and Saul put people at risk with their requests. Eliezer endangered Isaac; Caleb and Saul, their daughters. Their vows affected only human beings, while Jephthah's affected God directly, insulting him and calling forth his wrath.

The exegete makes his comparison on both planes: content and style, a comparison that once places Jephthah at the centre of the event, in the making of a vow that shows him as a crude ignoramus who does not respect the basic principles of belief in the God of Israel. This, says the Sage in the very beginning of the midrash, is the real reason for the terrible tragedy of sacrificing the daughter: Jephthah's wrong perception of God. We are distanced even at this point from any thought that God could have been involved in the event.

A comparison with Eliezer, Caleb and Saul clears these three men completely and censures Jephthah, taking us far away from the biblical stories.

As a matter of fact, Eliezer spoke in a way that could be interpreted as effrontery when he said to God, 'Let it come to pass that the damsel to whom I shall say, "Let down thy pitcher"...thou hast appointed for thy servant Isaac'. He seems to have told God what sign to give to enable him to choose the right maiden for his master, not relying on God himself to provide the sign. Caleb and Saul did not even ask for God's help. Jephthah, by contrast, showed religious zeal: he went into battle against the Ammonites after 'the spirit of the Lord came upon him', even making a vow 'unto the Lord' (Judg. 11.29).

10. *Lev. R.* (trans. J.J. Slotki; ed. H. Freedman; London: Soncino Press, 1961 [1939]).

Presenting Jephthah's vow as impudent and crude is, moreover, not compatible with the fact that other biblical makers of vows used similar formulations and were not punished. Jacob vowed: 'If God will be with me, and will keep me in this way that I go, and will give me bread to eat, and raiment to put on, So that I come again in peace to my father's house; then shall the lord be my God; And this stone, which I have set for a pillar, shall be God's house: and of all that thou shalt give me, surely I will give the tenth unto thee' (Gen. 28.20-22). Abraham relied on God to provide a fitting sacrifice when he said to Isaac: 'My son, God will provide himself a lamb for sacrifice' (Gen. 22.8). Why, then, could Jephthah not rely on God to guide events so that a suitable sacrifice would emerge from his house? Thus, in criticizing the vow, the commentator deliberately departs from the biblical story. He describes Jephthah as a crude man lacking respect for the God of Israel, so as to construct a new mold for the story, one that will embody his own intellectual direction.

This is what changes the daughter's going out to meet her father from a tragic event to a punishment for sin. Jephthah deserved punishment for his impudent vow, and God indeed punished him when he 'prepared his daughter for him'. (This matter will be discussed in detail later.)

Like the midrash in *Genesis Rabbah*, the midrash in *Tanḥuma* opens with a severe reprimand to Jephthah on the inadequate formulation of his vow. But it does not compare it with other vows, dealing rather with the reason that Jephthah came to formulate his vow in that despicable way.

According to the midrash in *Tanḥuma*, Jephthah's sin is ignorance. Jephthah is not a Torah scholar so he does not know how to make a vow. If he were a scholar he would know how to redeem a vow involving life and death. In this midrash, too, the daughter going out to meet her father is perceived as a drastic punishment imposed 'so that all who make vows will study the laws of pledges and oaths, so that they will not err in their vows'. The purpose of the punishment, then, is to teach others that vows involving human life cannot be redeemed save by a value in money.

> If a man makes a vow involving human life, as it is said, 'the fruit of the righteous is a tree of life; and he that winneth souls is wise' (Prov. 11). If a man is just, even though he is just and does not study the Torah, he has nothing. Rather the fruit of the just is the tree of life, means that since he is a Torah scholar he learns how to deal with human life, as it is said, wise is he who deals with human life. If he knows how to deal with vows regarding human life he learned it from the Torah, and if he

has no learning he has nothing. Thus it was with Jephthah the Gileadite, who because he was not a Torah scholar, lost his daughter when he was fighting Ammonites, in the hour when he made the vow: '…if thou shalt without fail deliver the children of Ammon into my hands, Then it shall be, that whatsoever cometh forth of the doors of my house shall surely be the Lord's and I will offer it up for a burnt offering'. In that hour the Lord was angry with him and he said, if a dog or a pig or a camel comes out of his house he would offer it up as a sacrifice to me? So he provided his daughter. Why? So that all who make vows will study the laws of pledges and oaths, and will not act mistakenly when they make vows.

To sum up: the Sage of *Genesis Rabbah* emphasizes Jephthah's sin, while the *Tanhuma* Sage stresses the reason for it. Both begin by taking a direction intended to remove the God of Israel from any possible link to human sacrifice, and both perceive the daughter's going out to meet her father as a deliberate punishment inflicted to teach a lesson.

This explanation raises difficult questions. First, why does God cause the perfectly innocent daughter to die for the father's sins? Secondly, how could the midrash authors have created a story in which God controls events in a way that leads to human sacrifice, when their entire purpose was to show that God could not have possibly been involved in such a terrible deed?

Having started in this direction, the authors had to continue in it so they could explain how events developed in a way that placed responsibility on Jephthah, and on him alone. Let us look at *Genesis Rabbah*:

> *And it came to pass, when he saw her, that he rent his clothes* (Judg. 11.35). R. Johanan and Resh Lakish disagree.[11] R. Johanan maintained: He was liable for her monetary consecration; Resh Lakish said: He was not even liable for her monetary consecration. For we learned: If one declared of an unclean animal or an animal with a blemish, 'Behold, let these be burnt-offerings', his declaration is completely null. If he declared: 'Let these be *for* a burnt-offering', they must be sold, and he brings a burnt-offering for their money.

Mishnah Temurah 5.6 declares that if a man says of an unclean or blemished animal that it is a sacrifice, 'his words are null and void' and he

---

11.   The disagreement between R. Johanan and Resh Lakish is presented in the language of the Mishnah, *Tem.* 5.6: 'If he said of an unclean animal or one with a blemish, it is a sacrifice, it is as if he said nothing. If he said, for a sacrifice, he sells it and brings a sacrifice for its money value'. In *Lev. R.* these words appear in paraphrase. *Yalquṭ Shim'oni* uses the same language as *Gen. R.* except for one place, in the beginning of Sign 68, Sign 67 having concluded with a dialogue between Jephthah and his daughter. In *Tanhuma* the whole passage is missing.

is under no obligation whatever to make 'a sacrifice'. If, however, he says it is 'for a sacrifice' he must sell it and bring a sacrifice for the price he received.

Jephthah said: 'whatsoever cometh forth from the doors of my house to meet me shall surely be the Lord's, and I will offer it up as a burnt-offering'. For that reason, according to the Mishnah, he was under no obligation to keep the vow. Nonetheless, according to R. Johanan who interpreted the passage more strictly in his commentary on the Mishnah, the man who said 'a sacrifice' had to pay his vow in money, and so Jephthah's obligation was to pay in money.

Presenting the dispute between R. Johanan and Resh Lakish, the author of the midrash once again shifts the blame for sacrificing the daughter onto Jephthah's shoulders. The Holy One, blessed be he, punished Jephthah by 'preparing his daughter for him', and that is how the punishment was to have ended. Its main component was to have been Jephthah's alarm when he saw his daughter. The divine plan seems to have been to frighten Jephthah so he would learn a lesson, that is, to teach the ignoramus by giving him a shock so he would see how foolish his vow was. God's purpose was 'to bray a fool in a mortar'[12] but not to go beyond that. Jephthah in his ignorance, however, did not know what to do because he was not a Torah scholar, combining sin with crime, and exacerbating the situation.

The commentator escalates his castigation of Jephthah. In the beginning, the formulation of the vow shows disrespect for God and disregard of an important tenet of belief. Later, his insistence on keeping his vow shows that he does not know the Law, the instrument through which faith is applied in daily life. In this part of the midrash another stratum is added, presenting Jephthah as the one solely responsible for sacrificing his daughter. God created the circumstances, but Jephthah could have changed them. He should have known what to do in the dilemma that God confronted him with, but did not and so brought the calamity upon himself.

In the next part of the midrash in *Genesis Rabbah* the author raises the castigation of Jephthah further. Up to this point Jephthah had failed in faith and in knowledge, but he still could have extricated himself, were it not for a flaw in his character. He could have done what any person would have done if he made a vow under stress, one that he could not keep, and asked the priest to release him from the vow. Thus the midrash in *Genesis Rabbah*:[13]

---

12. Prov. 27.22.
13. In *Lev. R.* and *Tanḥuma* the passage appears with minor changes, right after

Yet was not Phinehas there to absolve him of his vow? Phinehas, however, said: He needs me, and I am to go to him! Moreover, I am High Priest and the son of a High Priest; shall I then go to an ignoramus? While Jephthah said: Am I, the chief of Israel's leaders, to go to Phinehas! Between the two of them, the maiden perished. Thus people say: 'Between the midwife and the woman in travail the young woman's child is lost!' Both were punished for her blood. Jephthah died through his limbs dropping off: wherever he went a limb would drop off from him, and it was buried there on the spot. Hence it is written, *Then died Jephthah the Gildeadite, and was buried in the cities of Gilead.* It does not say, 'In a city of Gilead', but '*In the cities of Gilead*'. Phinehas was deprived of the divine inspiration. Hence it is written, *And Phinehas the son of Eleazar had been ruler over them* (1 Chron. 9.20): it is not written, He was ruler over them, but had been ruler in time past, [when] the Lord was with him (1 Chron. 9.20).

Jephthah, then, was guilty of another sin: lust for honour and power, which blinded him to his daughter's terrible distress, and hardened his heart so he could not even sense his own great sorrow. From now on, full responsibility for his daughter's death falls on Jephthah. In the first error, the crude wording of the vow may have been the result of stress. As for the second, perhaps Jephthah was not to blame that he had not been brought up on the foundations of faith and the study of the Law. But his lust for honour and power cannot be justified: it is an innate character defect. The supposed lust for honour and power is probably based on the biblical narrative, which relates that a condition of his going to war was that if he won, the Gileadites would make him their ruler: his words might have come from a heart heavy over what the Gileadites did to him in his youth, making him long now to control them.

In conclusion, the *Genesis Rabbah* midrash attributes three sins to Jephthah, arranging them and what causes Jephthah to sin, in a hierarchical order:

First sin	Wording of the vow	*Cause*	Flawed understanding of what faith means
Second sin	Intent to redeem the vow literally	*Cause*	Ignorance—flawed understanding of the Law
Third sin	Redeeming the vow	*Cause*	Lust for power and honour—flawed understanding of reality

'and the Holy One, Blessed be He answered him in an unfitting manner, and prepared his daughter for him. And when he saw her he rent his clothes...' In *Yalquṭ Shim'oni* the last two passages are in the same order as in *Gen. R.*

The gradations of severity stem from the sin itself: from the way the vow was worded, to the intent and to the preparation for carrying it out, and from the cause: from flaws that do not entirely depend on Jephthah himself but on circumstances and the way he was brought up, to that which is entirely within the man's own character. There is another gradation: the first sin is committed by Jephthah himself, where no outside force could have kept him from it; the second could have been prevented had he consulted a scholar; in the third he had a partner in transgression—Phinehas the High Priest—who, like Jephthah, in his moral blindness would not set his dignity aside.

The punishment hierarchy, in two stages only, is not entirely congruent with that of the transgression. The penalty for the first sin is that Jephthah's daughter comes out to meet him. For the second and third, Jephthah is punished by having his limbs fall off, and Phinehas by losing the divine inspiration.

Removing the daughter from the last two stages helps do away with any possibility of holding God responsible in any way for her death. This rests entirely on Jephthah and Phinehas, and God responds to the act that is entirely of human doing by punishing the two guilty parties.

The sense that the daughter is an instrument in God's hands to punish her father, which one gets from the first part of the midrash, disappears entirely in the last part. In the really serious part of the transgression the daughter is entirely out of the picture, and what happens to her has nothing to do with the divine plan for Jephthah.

In *Tanḥuma* there is no mention of Jephthah's ignorance of the Law. The first midrash has only two parts: (1) condemnation for the effrontery of the vow previously mentioned; (2) a description of the possibility of release from the vow with the help of Phinehas, which came to nothing because of the pride of the priest and of Jephthah.

> And behold, Jephthah's daughter came out to meet him, and when he saw her he rent his garments and said, Alas my daughter! Thou has brought me very low, and thou art one of them that trouble me; for I have opened my mouth unto the Lord and I cannot go back. Phinehas was there[14] and said 'I could not retract'. But what Phinehas said was 'I am the High Priest, son of a High Priest: how can I go to an ignorant man?' Jephthah said: 'I am the first Judge of Israel, chief of all the officers of its hosts. Shall I lower myself

---

14. In Judg. 20.27-28, in the story of the war with the Benjaminites after the affair of the woman in Gibeah: '...for the ark of the covenant of God was there in those days, And Phinehas, the son of Eleazar, the son of Aaron stood before it in those days'.

and go to an ordinary man?' Between the two, the hapless maiden was lost, and her blood was on their heads. Phinehas lost the divine spirit and Jephthah died as his body fell apart, limb by limb, as it is said, *He was buried in the cities of Gilead*.

There follows another midrash centred on the daughter.[15] It is different from the first midrash in content, and in the way it deals with God's link to the terrible act of the sacrifice, but similar in its escalation in the wickedness, and parallel to that, in the dimensions of the calamity.

Here too, three stages correspond to the three sections of the midrash. The first part is the dialogue between Jephthah and his daughter.

> When he sought to approach her she wept and said to him: 'My father, in joy I went out to meet you and you are going to slay me? Did the Holy One of Israel write in his Torah that human beings are to be offered up as sacrifices? It is written in the Torah that when a man sacrifices to God it shall be of the herd (Lev. 1) and not a human being!' He said: 'My daughter, I have vowed that whatsoever comes out to meet me, I shall offer it up as a burnt offering. Can one who has made a vow not redeem it?' She said: 'Jacob our father vowed of everything thou givest me… (Gen. 25), and God gave him twelve sons. He did not offer one of them up as a sacrifice to God! And Hannah also vowed and said, If the Lord of Hosts will look… (1 Sam. 1), and did she offer her son up as a sacrifice to God?' All these things she told him and he did not heed her.

The dialogue itself , like the midrash, is constructed in hierarchical fashion, in three stages that emphasise the three flaws of Jephthah: misunderstanding of faith, ignorance of the Law and lust after honour, as set forth in *Genesis Rabbah*. While the content of the first stage is based on Jephthah's monologue in the Bible, the midrash presents it as a dialogue between father and daughter, expanding and reinforcing it with suggestions from the Bible.

In the Bible Jephthah says: 'Then it shall be that whatsoever cometh forth from the doors of my house to meet me when I return in peace…'

In the midrash, the daughter answers him: 'Father, in joy I went out to meet you and you are going to slay me?' (The word 'slay' recurs many times in the midrash, a point I shall discuss later.)

In the Bible Jephthah says: 'shall surely be the Lord's, and I will offer it up for a burnt offering'.

---

15. The first part of the second midrash in *Tanḥuma* appears as well in *Yalquṭ Shim'oni*, Judges 67: the last part of the second midrash in *Tanḥuma* is also in *Ta'anit* 4a.

In the midrash the daughter answers, 'Did the Holy One of Israel write in his Torah that human beings are to be offered up as sacrifices? It is written in the Torah that when a man sacrifices to God it shall be of the herd (Lev. 1) and not a human being!'

In the Bible Jephthah says: 'I have opened my mouth unto the Lord and I cannot go back'. And the daughter answers him: 'My father, if thou has opened thy mouth unto the Lord, do to me according to that which has proceeded from thy mouth...'

In the midrash the daughter answers with a series of proofs that a vow like his need not be redeemed. 'She said to him Jacob our father vowed, "Of everything thou has given me...and God gave him twelve sons". He did not offer one of them up as a sacrifice to God! Hannah vowed and said, "O Lord of Hosts, if thou wilt indeed look on the affliction of thine handmaid, and remember me, and not forget thine handmaid, but wilt give unto thine handmaid a man child, then I will give him to the Lord" (1 Sam. 1). Did she offer her son up as a sacrifice to the Lord?'

In the daughter's series of historical proofs there are hints of irony against Jephthah, who displayed such broad historical knowledge in his argument with the Ammonite king but suddenly forgot everything that might have saved his daughter. Perhaps, however, placing additional blame on Jephthah for his selective memory is an even stronger element than the irony.

The hierarchy in the midrashic dialogue is clear: In the first stage the daughter makes an emotional plea in response to Jephthah's 'Alas, my daughter! Thou hast brought me very low'. The daughter expresses her terrible shock in the stark contrast of '*My father*, in *joy* I went out to meet you and you are going to *slay* me!'

In the second stage the daughter's plea is based on faith, and on understanding the spirit of the Torah. The daughter is seen as an intelligent believer, while her father stands before her as a stupid believer who does not understand the very essence of belief.

And as in the first stage of the first midrash, Jephthah worded his vow in a completely flawed understanding of belief, so in the second stage of this midrash he insists on redeeming his vow in the light of that flaw.

The third stage of the daughter's plea is based on knowledge. She brings examples from the history of Israel to prove to her father that he can keep his vow without offering her up as a sacrifice. His failure to respond shows him not only as ignorant, but also as one who does not let himself hear or listen. By contrast with the knowledge he displayed when arguing with the Ammonite king, the ignorance and obstinacy in his encounter with his daughter are grave indeed.

Here ends the first part of the second midrash. Followed by several lines telling how the daughter sought help from the Sages of the Sanhedrin, it forms a transition to the second part.

> Since she saw that her father did not heed her she said to him, 'Let me go down to the court where perchance a release may be found from your vow', as it is said (Judges 11), *Let me alone two months that I may* [literal translation] *go down on the mountains*... Said Rabbi Zechariah, Does anyone go down on the mountains: people go up on the mountains. What is 'I may go down on the mountains' except [going to] the Sanhedrin, as it is said (Micah 6), *Hear ye, O mountains the Lord's controversy.*

These lines show the daughter to be knowledgeable about the procedure for release from vows, an active personality and an initiator ready to go to the ends of the earth to find a solution. The father is shown in a negative light, a passive individual who, according to the first midrash, would not go to Phinehas because he would not swallow his own pride.

In structuring these lines, the Sage of the midrash takes advantage of the dichotomy in the daughter's words in the biblical narrative. Twice there appear the words 'and she said'. The first time (v. 36), 'And she said unto him, "My father, if thou hast opened thy mouth unto the Lord, do to me according to that which proceeded out of thy mouth; forasmuch as the Lord hath taken vengeance for thee of thine enemies, even of the children of Ammon"'. In the second instance (v. 37) the words are: 'And she said unto her father, "Let this thing be done for me: let me alone two months, that I may go down among the mountains..."'. The midrash ignores the daughter's first words and begins the second section with what she says the second time. However, it makes a hidden assumption that, between the first and second times she spoke, a terrible deed took place, the massacre of the Ephraimites, for which Jephthah was responsible. The daughter's going to the mountains, according to the interpretation of the midrash, means going to the Sanhedrin to seek a way out—a release from the vow. The midrashic author combines the strange words 'down on the mountains...' with another strange text in Micah 6, 'Hear ye, O mountains the Lord's controversy'. From this he concludes that the word 'mountains' carries another meaning: an assembly of Sages, in other words, the Sanhedrin.

Here the author does something extraordinary: he returns God to the scene of the action, and appears to mar the structure over which he laboured so hard up to this point, in the attempt to distance God from any hint of involvement in the sacrifice of the daughter.

In punishment for Jephthah's terrible sin, which according to the midrash took place between the two dialogues with the daughter, God hides the law from the Sages of the Sanhedrin.

The midrash assumes that the massacre of the Ephraimites took place before the daughter went to the Sanhedrin. The assumption appears to rest on the two openings 'and she said', indicating two dialogues between her and her father. This made it possible for the midrashic author to assume the passage of time during which the murderous act described in Judges 11 took place, while the Bible does not place it in a particular time sequence.

> She went to them and they found no opening for Jephthah, no way to release him from his vow, because of his sin in slaying the Ephraimites. Of him it is said (Prov. 28), *A poor man that oppresseth the poor is like a sweeping rain that leaveth no bread*. The poor man that oppresseth the poor is Jephthah who was poor in learning like the poor man who oppressed the poor, as it is said (Judges 12), *Say now Shibboleth and he said Sibboleth*, for he could not pronounce it right. Then they took him and slew him at the passages of the Jordan. Thus he was like a driving rain that leaveth no food, and there was no one left to release him from his vow, because God hid the law from them and they found no way to release him.

In some midrashim, 'bread' means Torah. Thus, in Prov. 9.5, when Wisdom says 'Come eat of my bread', Torah is the intent. That the Law has been hidden from the Sanhedrin Sages is a difficult idea indeed, unless Jephthah by his crime against the Ephraimites has driven away the food that is Torah. Now the divine punishment makes it truly impossible for the Sages to provide Jephthah with a release from his vow, and so he sacrifices his daughter.

However, it seems to me that this too may be understood in the same way as the daughter's going out to meet her father, in the first midrash. Just as there, the daughter going out to meet him was to have shocked Jephthah and to make him understand that his vow was invalid, so concealing the law from the members of the Sanhedrin was to have shocked Jephthah into an understanding of the enormity of his act against the Ephraimites—certainly not to make him sacrifice his daughter.

There are difficulties in interpreting the concealment of the law as a punishment designed to shock, in the situation that this midrash describes, since Jephthah is not at the Sanhedrin with his daughter. Still, it is possible to assume that the midrash author meant that Jephthah would be shocked when his daughter returned from the Sanhedrin and told him that the court had found no solution, thus making him understand the horror of the calamity and perhaps prevent it.

A recurring motif in the midrash is that God hides the Law from humans as a punishment intended to teach a lesson, and to force them to find alternative solutions. For example: the midrash in the Babylonian Talmud, *Tem.* 16a, relates that Joshua angered and insulted Moses by not responding to his request, 'Ask me about any doubts you have', on the grounds that he had already learned everything, since he never left Moses' tent. In punishment, 'His strength failed immediately and he forgot three hundred laws and there arose within him seven hundred doubts, and all Israel was about to kill him'. The solution that freed Joshua from the people's wrath was, 'Go busy them with a war'. Similarly, when Moses himself refused to die, God hid the Law from him. He sat among the last of the scholars and did not understand what was being taught: 'Moses did not know what Joshua was explaining'. He then became reconciled to his death and said, 'Lord of the World, until now I asked for life and now I render my soul to you' (*Tanḥuma, Ve-Ethanan* 6). Another midrash describes it somewhat differently:

> When the pillar of cloud [that separated Moses from Joshua] departed, Moses went to Joshua and asked him, 'And what was the Word to you?' Joshua answered him: 'And when the Word was revealed to you, did I know what it said?' In that hour Moses shouted, 'A hundred deaths rather than envy once' (*Deut. R.* 9.5).

The punishment of concealing the Law from the Sanhedrin Sages was intended, then, to shock Jephthah, to expose him once again to the horror of choosing to take a life, and have him make good the damage he had done. But Jephthah did not understand that the punishments were intended to make him confront the situation and choose, so he 'went up and slew her'.

With this phrase the author goes on to the third and last part of the midrash—God's reaction.

> And the Holy Spirit shouted, Did I want you to sacrifice human lives to me? Spake I not unto your fathers nor commanded them, nor came it into my heart (Jer. 7). I commanded not Abraham to slay his son, but rather Lay not thine hand upon the lad, to tell all the nations of the world of Abraham's love, who did not withhold his only son from me, to do the will of his Creator. I did not tell Jephthah to sacrifice his daughter, nor came it into my heart that Mesha king of Moab,[16] as it is

16. In *Ta'anit* the order is reversed: '*Which I commanded not, nor spake it, neither came it to my mind*. "*Which I commanded not*": this refers to the sacrifice of the son of

written (2 Kings 3) fell into the hand of the king of Israel, then he took
his eldest son that should have reigned in his stead and offered him up
for a burnt offering. It was asked, who caused Mesha to sacrifice his son:
because he knew not the Torah, because if he had read the Torah he
would not have destroyed his son as it is written in the Torah, If a man
make a singular vow, the persons shall be for the Lord by thy estimation. And thy estimation shall be of the male from twenty years old
even unto sixty years old, even thy estimation shall be fifty shekels of
silver...(Lev. 27.1). He that winneth souls is wise.

This section too is constructed in three hierarchical stages, in which
the midrash Sage makes a supreme effort to render it entirely unthinkable that God should have had anything to do with Jephthah's terrible
deed.

From the Holy Spirit three cries go forth: 'I did not command, I did
not speak, and it came not into my heart' (Jer. 7). Each cry is an additional stage in removing God from a perception that makes human
sacrifice possible.

In the first cry 'I did not command', in the language of the biblical
stories about Abraham and Jephthah, there is a hint of the similarity
between the situations in which Abraham and Jephthah found themselves. In Gen. 22.2 Abraham is told, 'Take now thy son, thine only
son'. In Judg. 11.34 the writer says of Jephthah's daughter 'and she
was his only child'.

But conceivably, someone might imagine that God prevented Abraham from sacrificing his only son and did not prevent Jephthah from
sacrificing his only daughter because he loved Abraham, and not because, in principle, he detested human sacrifices. Hence the second
cry 'I did not speak', which relates to Jephthah. He does not walk with
God as Abraham did, but still God did not command him to sacrifice
his daughter ('Speak' has the force of command here). But even so,
someone might imagine that while God did not want human sacrifices from among his own people he would desire them from the
heathen who follow this custom. This is the reason for the third cry, 'It
did not come into my heart', pointing to Mesha king of Moab who
sacrificed his son in vain: had he known the laws of Israel he would
have sacrificed the *value* of his son, following the procedure the Torah
sets forth to deal with a person's need to consecrate human beings to

Mesha, the king of Moab, as it is said, *Then he took his eldest son that should have
reigned in his stead and offered him for a burnt-offering.* "*Nor spake it*"; This refers to the
daughter of Jephthah. "*Neither came it into my mind*": This refers to the sacrifice of
Isaac, the son of Abraham'.

God. This, then, ends the discussion of the three parts of the second midrash in *Tanḥuma*.

Comparing the two *Tanḥuma* midrashim reveals a symmetric structure whose purpose is to reveal Jephthah's wickedness stage by stage, presenting him as a terrible criminal. In parallel fashion, stage by stage, it distances from the reader the thought that God could have any possible connection with human sacrifice, so that such an idea can be eliminated altogether.

In the first midrash, Jephthah's character develops parallel to his sin, as I have described earlier. First, he is presented as a crude man whose sin is not knowing how to formulate his vow. After that he is shown to lust after honour and authority, along with another man of the same type, Phinehas, a sin that led to the loss of a human soul. In this midrash, Jephthah's sin in the first part is a *mistaken vow*, and in the second, *destroying life*.

In the second midrash, too, there is escalation. The character of Jephthah, and his sin, develop in ways that make them much more extreme. In the beginning he is shown as a vulgar, ignorant, unheeding man, and the last quality develops to a degree that turns him into a mass murderer, whose deeds climax in the murder of his only daughter. In this midrash the sin is defined from the first stage as *slaying*. Meeting her father, the daughter says to him, 'You slay me'. In the second stage there is mass slaying. Jephthah is punished 'for the sin of slaying the Ephraimites'. The final development, in the third stage, is the *slaying of his daughter*: in the language of the midrash itself, 'went up and slew her'.

One notes that throughout, in relating to Jephthah, the midrashic writer uses the word 'slay', while in relation to God 'sacrifice' is used. There is one exception: 'I did not command Abraham to slay his son'. However, one supposes the word was used here because of its closeness to the language of the Bible (Gen. 22.10): 'And Abraham stretched forth his hand, and took the knife to slay his son', before the continuation, 'Lay not thine hand upon the lad' (v. 12).

To sum up: The two *Tanḥuma* midrashim, like the midrash in *Genesis Rabbah*, deliberately have Jephthah's character growing blacker before our eyes as we read. And the blacker it gets, the greater God's revulsion from human sacrifice becomes. In all the midrashim, Jephthah sins and is punished: thus God's intervention ends and the choice lies with Jephthah. He could make the situation worse or find a way out. The midrashim show a series of possibilities, he fails in every instance and so, instead of emerging from calamity and sin, he sinks in ever deeper.

The reader of the midrash is convinced that Jephthah forced the calamity on himself and on his daughter, electing to slay her. The whole story begins with a mistaken vow, continues with his obstinate intent to carry it out, and concludes with the daughter's death, which is entirely Jepthah's own distorted decision. God has no hand in the deed, except for presenting the dilemma[17] that forced the choice. In anger and sorrow, God watched events unfold but did not guide them.

Still a problem —

---

17. Jonah Frankel, *Darchei Ha-Aggadah ve-ha-Midrash* (*Paths in the Aggadah and the Midrash*) (Israel: Massada, 1991), p. 243, writes: 'Generally speaking, you will not find a Bible hero from whom God's word is hidden, and so he himself has to find what God wants of him'. By contrast, says Frankel, heroes of the *Aggadah* (who are of course Bible heroes in midrashic dress) have to find out God's word, which confronts them with dilemmas.

JEPHTHAH'S DAUGHTER: A THEMATIC APPROACH TO THE NARRATIVE AS SEEN IN SELECTED RABBINIC EXEGESIS AND IN ARTWORK

Phyllis Silverman Kramer

A. *Introduction*

The use of art for biblical interpretation both as religious images and as less religious statements has spanned many centuries. Iconographic representations play an important and meaningful role in biblical exegesis. Evaluating this artwork can serve as an interpretive aid in Bible study, since artistic renderings provide images and clues as to how a biblical figure will be visualized and remembered. The figures themselves, their placement within the artwork, the colors, tones and shadings, and the scenic background are each important to the overall feeling and sense of how an artist depicts a narrative. Allowing for varied and varying interpretations, the viewer should be able to see a connection between the Bible text and the work of art. Although the artist might manipulate the biblical narrative while creating her or his work, the viewer should expect reasonable harmony between the text and the art. Text-affiliated interpretation should be evident.

A biblical story that has received artistic attention is the story of Jephthah's daughter. From stylized, simplistic drawings to powerful, commanding paintings, this tragic story has evoked iconographic creativity. One would expect to find in the artwork the tremendous range of emotions read in the Bible. In this narrative, artists are able to focus on the two main protagonists. Additionally, the combinations of male–female and father–daughter heightens interest and appeal.

The narrative may be divided into mini-scenes or vignettes, and the art reflects this thematic approach: (1) Jephthah's daughter greeting her father upon his arrival home; (2) the daughter lamenting her maidenhood with her friends; and (3) the sacrifice of the daughter.

B. *Jephthah's Daughter in the Bible*

Appearing in the book of Judges (11.34-40) is one of many unnamed females in Scripture, a young girl known only by her kinship with her father and called simply 'Jephthah's daughter'. Her story, one of the saddest in the Bible despite its narrative terseness of seven verses, still offers a description of her, insight into her personality, her acceptance of her destiny and the development of a custom arising from her circumstance and memory.

Jephthah had made a vow to God that, if he returned home victorious from battle, he would offer as a sacrifice whatever exited first from his home to greet him. It was his only child, the unnamed daughter, who came out with timbrels and dances to meet him. In anguish, he rent his garments and chastised her for the grief she caused him because of his irrevocable pledge to God. In innocence or respect or compliance, she did not challenge him to save her life; rather, she was acquiescent and affirmed the necessity of his executing his oath. Jephthah's daughter had only one request, a two-month period to go off with her friends to the mountains to bewail what appears at first glance to be her virginity. Her father granted her wish and, upon her return from the mountains, he fulfilled his vow.

Jephthah's promise to God and the resulting death of his daughter evoke questions: could Jephthah, when he made the vow, not have cared what the sacrifice would be? Was he more concerned with victory than the object of his vow? Was his vow irrevocable?

A personality trait Jephthah's daughter demonstrated to an exaggerated degree was acquiescence. Having learned she was to be a human sacrifice, she did not beseech her father to save her nor offer an alternate plan. Why did she not counter her father when he blamed her for the tragic circumstance? Was she meek? Fatalistic? Accepting of her fate at any personal cost? She was to be sacrificed, yet he castigated her!

In this episode, the societal importance of bearing a child was clear when Jephthah's daughter took time to bewail her maidenhood—to mourn the fact she would never have a child. It makes no sense that her virginity is the issue, that she would want to go off and bewail her virginity, which could be easily rectified. Also, she did not choose to go off in solitude, but rather to solemnize the tragic circumstances with her companions who would offer her compassion and support. The power of her prayer was to be shared with friends in a location conducive to a theological or faith experience. Then, having gone to mourn her maidenhood with her friends and knowing she would die a virgin, she was prepared to give up her life.

C. *Jephthah's Daughter in Rabbinic Interpretation and Other Post-Biblical Jewish Sources*

1. *Jephthah Returns Home (v. 34)*

Pseudo-Philo[1] presented an expanded, scintillating version of the biblical story by adding accessory people, supplementary information which presented a picture of the time in which Jephthah lived, and more emotional descriptions. He named Jephthah's daughter Seila. The community's taciturn reaction to the vow, and the young daughter's priorities, add to the questioning of how such a travesty could have happened.

When Jephthah returned, writes *Pseudo-Philo*, not only his daughter came out to greet him but 'women' (40.1) also came. It was specified that his daughter was the first to exit to greet him. While numerous people would assuredly greet and honor the victorious warrior, only the presence of his daughter was noted.[2]

Josephus wrote that when his daughter exited her home to greet him, Jephthah 'chid his daughter for her haste in meeting him, seeing that he had dedicated her to God'; and described her as being compliant, 'for she without displeasure learnt her destiny, to wit that she must die in return for her father's victory and the liberation of her fellow-citizens'.[3] Once again, an exegetical remark centers on the daughter's lack of resistance to try and save her own life.

2. *The Reactions of Jephthah and his Daughter (vv. 35-36)*

In responding to his daughter's salutation, wrote *Pseudo-Philo*, Jephthah did not tear his garments; rather, he expressed his anguish by swooning and addressing her by name: 'Rightly was your name Seila, that you might be offered in sacrifice. And now who will put my

---

1.   All references will be found in *OTP*, II, pp. 353-54. The fulsome inclusion of *Pseudo-Philo*'s commentary is presented since his rendition of Jephthah's daughter influences *The Chronicles of Jerahmeel*; or *The Hebrew Bible Historiale* (New York: Ktav, 1971) and is evident in Louis Ginzberg's *The Legends of the Jews* (7 vols.; Philadelphia: Jewish Publication Society of America, 1913), IV, pp. 43-47.

2.   It was a natural occurrence for women to rejoice in song at victorious moments in the history of the Israelites: cf. Exod. 15.20, where Miriam led the women after the Israelites' victorious crossing of the Red Sea, and 1 Sam. 18.6-7, where women feted David after he arrived home triumphant.

3.   Josephus, *Ant.* 5.5-8.

heart in the balance and my soul on the scale? And I will stand by and see which will win out, whether it is the rejoicing that has occurred or the sadness that befalls me' (40.1). In other words, he had to fulfill his vow. Altschuler (Metzudat Zion) translated הכרע הכרעתני as 'kneeling and falling'.[4] Perhaps the father swooned as he saw the daughter coming to greet him.

Seila, countering her father's reaction by saying his victory for his people was of primary importance, asked if he remembered that, in the history of the ancestors, a son willingly was offered 'as a holocaust, and he did not refuse him but gladly gave consent to him, and the one being offered was ready and the one who was offering was rejoicing' (40.2). So, too, must her father do to her. So, too, she has capitulated.

A singular picture of Jephthah's daughter fighting for her life was apparent in Midrash Tanḥuma where she argued with her father, citing biblical proof for his not being compelled to sacrifice her. She cited how Jacob vowed to give a tithe of all he had to God, yet never sacrificed any of his children (Gen. 28.20-22), and remarked about Hannah having vowed to dedicate her son to God but not sacrificing his life (1 Sam. 1.11).[5]

Jephthah's anguished reaction to his daughter's greeting expressed joy turned to grief, public victory into personal disaster. What the enemy did not achieve, his daughter now had accomplished by depriving him of joy and causing him disaster (40.1). Jephthah's reaction to her welcome was the exegetical focus of this verse. He berated her for his grief, feeling he could not renege on his well-intentioned vow.

3. *A Request Is Made and Granted (vv. 37-38)*
The Bible indicated that the daughter went to the mountains for the prescribed time period; *Exodus Rabbah* (15.5) claimed she went to the elders to show them she was a pure virgin.[6] Rashi also stated, based

---

4.   A.J. Rosenberg (ed.), *Judges: A New Translation* (New York: The Judaica Press, 1987), p. 102.

5.   *Midrash Tanḥuma, Sefer Vayikra* (Williamsburg: Me'ein Ha-Torah, 1963), p. 139. See Shulamit Valler, 'The Story of Jephthah's Daughter in the Midrash', pp. 48-66 in this volume, for references made in this essay to *Ta'anit, Gen. R., Tanḥuma* and *Lev. R.*

6.   Cf. *Hārîm*, found in SoS 2.8, means mountains; however, the word has a range of unrelated connotations, allowing for multiple interpretations. Mic. 6.2, in using *hārîm*, alluded to the Sanhedrin while Zech. 6.1 meant idol worshippers. In *Roš Haš.* 11b, mountains and hills refer to the Patriarchs and Matriarchs, respec-

on *Tanḥuma* (בחקת 5),[7] that Jephthah's daughter went to the San-hedrin on the mountain to see if a different solution could be found for her father's promise. She wished to go away in the company of her friends so she could talk about the pain of not having borne a child. Radak, reiterating what Rashi had said about the Sanhedrin, was concerned with the geographical location of the mountains, not with her personal needs, request and emotions.

In *Pseudo-Philo's* version Seila asked to be allowed to go to the mountains with her 'virgin companions' (40.3); however, she did not specify a length of time. Here *Pseudo-Philo* amplified the text, having Jephthah's daughter express her emotions:

> I will pour out my tears there and tell of the sadness of my youth. And the trees of the field will weep for me, and the beasts of the field will lament over me. For I am not sad because I am to die nor does it pain me to give back my soul, but because my father was caught up in the snare of his vow; and if I did not offer myself willingly for sacrifice, I fear that my death would not be acceptable or I would lose my life in vain (40.3).

Her deep concern that the fulfillment of the vow be proper is of major import. Her total submission seems at variance with nature mourning so deeply for her.

Pseudo-Philo proposed the most extraordinary comment about what happened to Seila on the mountain. He suggested she had a theo-phany during which God thought of her by night and said,

> Behold now I have shut up the tongue of the wise men of my people for this generation so that they cannot respond to the daughter of Jephthah, to her word, in order that my word be fulfilled and my plan that I thought out not be foiled. And I have seen that the virgin is wise in contrast to her father and perceptive in contrast to all the wise men who are here. And now let her life be given at his request, and her death will be precious before me always, and she will go away and fall into the bosom of her mothers (40.4).

Pseudo-Philo's assertion that Jephthah's daughter was spoken to by God was unique; his intimation that God was the motivating force be-hind her death was astonishing. To think that God, recognizing her wisdom and perceptiveness, could orchestrate the wise men and be the primary mover in causing a needless death is cause for serious study.

---

tively. Targum Jonathan asserted that the mountains which were leapt and skipped over referred to years lessened in servitude for the Children of Israel in Egypt.

7. *Midrash Tanḥuma* (Jerusalem: Lewin-Epstein, 1964).

Midrashic sources focused on the request Jephthah's daughter made to go away for two months. In *The Chronicles of Jerahmeel* the author posited that she wanted to go off with her companions to 'shed my tears and thus soften the grief of my youth'.[8] She was submissive about her father's vow, but felt she might not be worthy. God gave her assurance 'her death shall be very precious in My sight'.[9] At this point, an attitude change by Jephthah's daughter surfaced: Seila 'fell upon her mother's bosom'[10] and went to lament her faith. This commentary offered a singular approach about the daughter's feelings, positing she showed antagonism toward her father. In crying to her mother she shared heartbreaking descriptions of her sadness, and evoked compassion and mourning from her companions as well as from the trees (cf. *Ps.-Philo* 40.6-7). This source said she went to lament her faith rather than her fate.

Judges 11.37 is a request made in the first person by Jephthah's daughter. In the request to her father to grant her two months to go to the mountains with her friends, Rashi interpreted the word וירדתי (lit. 'go down') as signifying not simply lamenting but rather a tremendous sadness, as though one's body was breaking. He put the word וירדתי into the context of mourning and explained that she descended to an emotional state that resulted in crying, citing a prooftext where people went on the roof tops and out on the streets wailing, with tears streaming and their bodies breaking because their sobbing was so hard (Isa. 15.30). Altschuler posited that the daughter shall cry over her virginity because she 'will not be able to marry anyone. Crying helps lessen and relieve the pain'.[11]

Verse 38 offered a closure on verse 37 as Jephthah granted permission to his daughter to leave. Given the several component parts of this verse, it was disappointing not to find more interpretive focus on Jephthah's daughter. Neither was there any examination nor speculation about who her friends were, and what they actually did during the time they were absent.

4. *The Vow is Fulfilled; a Custom Is Established (vv. 39-40)*
After the sojourn on the mountain, *Pseudo-Philo* wrote, Jephthah's daughter 'returned to her father, and he did everything that he had

8.   *The Chronicles of Jerahmeel*, p. 177.
9.   *The Chronicles of Jerahmeel*, p. 178.
10. *The Chronicles of Jerahmeel*, p. 178.
11. Rosenberg, *Judges*, p. 103.

vowed and offered the holocausts' (40.8).[12] Commenting on v. 39, Targum Jonathan exhorted Israel never to give a child sacrifice. Further explanation faulted Jephthah for not having gone to Phineas the priest who would have found a substitute sacrifice. This scathing commentary attested to the wrongness of Jephthah's act, as well as to the personality flaws he displayed.

Rabbi Yosef Kimchi, in commenting on v. 31, where Jephthah made his vow, is in the minority as he adds insight to the thought that Jephthah did not sacrifice his daughter. In commenting on the word והעליתיהו ('I shall offer it up', v. 31), Kimchi interprets the waw in this word disjunctively (cf. Exod. 21.17); thus, the verse means: 'If [a person] comes out, he [she] will be dedicated to God [i.e. to God's service], but if an animal comes out, I will offer it as a burnt-offering'. (Jephthah presumably had the right to dedicate his children or servants to God's service.)[13] This explanation makes a distinction between a person and an animal, and the appropriateness of different sacrifice measures to deal with each. If only Jephthah had been aware of the waw, he would have found an alternate sacrifice to offer.

Josephus was unequivocal in castigating Jephthah and stating that he 'sacrificed his child as a burnt-offering—a sacrifice neither sanctioned by the law nor well-pleasing to God; for he had not by reflection probed what might befall or in what aspect the deed would appear to them that heard of it'.[14]

An indictment of Jephthah's deed, found in the Babylonian Talmud (*Ta'an.* 4a), avowed that he should never have sacrificed his daughter. Scriptural prooftexts were cited to show God would never demand nor expect a human sacrifice. The biblical citations upholding the opinion that Jephthah erred dreadfully were: the aborted sacrifice of Isaac by his father Abraham (Gen. 22.11-18); God's extreme wrath against Mesha, King of Moab, who offered his son as a burnt offering (2 Kgs 3.27); and a reference to Jer. 8.22 and 19.5, where human sacrifice was condemned by God who had never commanded, spoken or even thought about such a heinous deed. *Ta'anit* 4a also included the opinion that the daughter's life could have been saved, had Phineas been asked to judge the situation. Additionally, God was angered because Jephthah did not go to Phineas to absolve him from his vow and

---

12. In the discussion of the artwork this paper will concentrate on v. 39, since it is the focus of this work .

13. Yaakov Elman, *The Living Nach: Early Prophets* (Jerusalem: Moznaim, 1994), p. 142.

14. Josephus, *Ant.* 5.

annul it. Castigation against Jephthah and Phineas was also rife in two other midrashim: Jephthah would not approach the High Priest, Phineas would not deign to go to Jephthah to give him counsel, and so the daughter was sacrificed (*Gen. R.* 60.3 and *Lev. R.* 37.4). The implication was they were held accountable for her death.

Two opposing views exist about how Jephthah fulfilled his vow (v. 39). The first was that he in fact put his daughter on the altar as a burnt offering (*Ta'an.* 4a, *Gen. R.* 70, Josephus). Jephthah had promised to sacrifice what turned out to be his daughter and did as he had vowed. She was the same status at her death as she was when the vow was made. There is an implication that, if she had married during the two-month reprieve, she would no longer be sacrificed. Her husband could have legally prevented her fate (Altschuler). A decree arose as a result of Jephthah having sacrificed his daughter, stipulating that no one would ever again do such a deed (Rashi).

In *Ta'an.* 4a a discussion affirms that God never wants a child sacrifice. This source implies that Jephthah did sacrifice his daughter. The prooftext is Jer. 19.5, which speaks about children offered as burnt sacrifices to Baal.

Another exegetical comment agrees that Jephthah did sacrifice his daughter:

> How, then, was it possible that a righteous person like Jephthah make such a horrendous mistake? Some say he was influenced by the idolatrous practices of his time. The Jews had become so steeped in idolatry that even when they turned to God, they worshipped Him with the abominable ceremonies of the pagan deities. The sacrifice of children seemed completely natural and acceptable to the Jews of that generation. Neither Jephthah nor his daughter even thought of questioning it. In their eyes it was the ultimate act of faith and dedication.[15]

The second point of view was that Jephthah did not sacrifice his daughter. This interpretation of what transpired was a fascinating variant, differing drastically from the prevalent targumic and midrashic thinking which judged Jephthah harshly for the terrible sacrificial act he had performed. Several medieval commentators held that no vow on a son or daughter could have been made (Ramban); rather, Jephthah made a special house for his daughter and put her into solitary confinement (Radak, Ralbag, and Abravanel). She spent the rest of her

15. S. Yerushalmi, *The Book of Judges: Me'am Lo'ez* (Jerusalem: Moznaim, 1991), p. 243.

life in seclusion, dedicated to the service of God (Radak). During the two months she was away with her companions, she looked for a place where she would live in seclusion. The idea of women going off to lament over Jephthah's daughter taught of the existence of cloisters, or places of abstinence, where women lived without ever seeing any male (Ralbag and Abravanel). The daughter's situation was likened to the Pharisees who remained secluded (Radak).

Abravanel and Radak strengthened their point of view by asserting that Jephthah's original words should be understood not as 'whatever goes out first from the doors of my house...will be for the Lord, *and* I will offer it as a sacrifice', but as '*or* I will offer it as a sacrifice'. If it were something that was appropriate to sacrifice, then he would sacrifice it. Otherwise, he would dedicate it to God.[16]

The final argument mitigating against the sacrifice was based on the daughter's words in v. 37, 'I will bewail my virginity'. Had she thought her life was to be sacrificed she would have referred to her life, not her virginity. Since she bewailed her virginity, it implied that she would live but remain unmarried as she was dedicated to God (Radak and Abravanel).

D. *A Study of Jephthah's Daughter in Art as an Exegetical Form*

In amassing the art works on Jephthah's daughter,[17] the images fell clearly into categories. As mentioned earlier, three themes predominate: Jephthah's return and meeting of his daughter;[18] her time on the mountains;[19] and her sacrifice or non-sacrifice.[20] The daughter's greeting of her father, and her time on the mountaintop with her friends, provide interpretation that mirrors the *peshat* closely. As seen in rabbinic exegesis, the only controversial segment of this narrative is

---

16. Yerushalmi, *Judges*, p. 243.

17. Each of the artworks not reproduced in this article can be found listed in the Appendix, together with a source book where it can be seen and the museum or collection where the original work is kept.

18. *The Pamplona Bible*; French artist c. 1250; Anonymous c. 1478/Quentell; German miniature; Stephan Fridolin; Anonymous 1485/ Johann (Reinhard) Grüninger; Jost Amman; Virgil Solis; Betsy B. Lathrop; Gustav Doré; Anonymous Woodcut; Gian Antonio Pellegrine; Tobias Stimmer.

19. French Artist c. 1250; Gustav Doré.

20. *The Pamplona Bible*; French Artist c. 1250; Anonymous 1473/Günther Zainer; Anonymous 1476/Anton Sorg; Anonymous 1476/Bernhard Richel; Peter Drach.

found in v. 39. The two schools of thought involve whether Jephthah did or did not actually offer his daughter as a sacrifice to God. Studying the images will enlighten us as to how several artists interpret this verse. I shall examine the visual variations that either mirror or contradict the *peshat* as well as details of physical objects and emotional responses. Finally, an investigation will be made of the images in the third category—that is, the sacrifice of Jephthah's daughter.

1. *Theme One: Jephthah's Return* (figure 1).
According to the verses listed in the title of this work,[21] this image portrays Jephthah crying to his daughter that she has brought him low because of his vow to God, and her response that he must do as he had promised. The image that accompanies the following description is a study for the painting. It is a brush drawing in brown wash, heightened with white graphite. The description below is based on the final (completed) work.

Three groups of figures are depicted: two on the left, three plus one in the center, and seven on the right. Left to right: a youngster exiting left is holding a frond. The upper part of his torso is naked. In front, going to the right is an architectural column in front of a male figure seated on a cushion in lotus position, hands holding his legs. This male looks upward. Perhaps the next image evokes the greatest emotional response on the part of the viewer. It is the only image in which physical contact, in the form of a heart-rending embrace, is drawn. To the left of center Jephthah is seated on a chair with his daughter in his lap. His head is dejectedly down. His sandalled right leg is bare of clothing and his garments are made of fur. A shield rests against the chair upon which he sits. His daughter, with full light focused on her, looks sadly downward. She wears a short-sleeved long dress and has a tiara on her long hair. Her right arm embraces her father. Her left hand holds his right hand which he holds up near his heart. His left hand surrounds her hand which is around his neck. Behind them, seen laterally, is a tall male figure with right arm outstretched on a curtain. Right of center is a crouching figure that looks sadly up at Jephthah's daughter. She and the figure behind the two protagonists appear to be negroid in their color and features. Her hair is covered by a mantilla,

21. W. Shaw Sparrow, *The Old Testament in Art: From the Creation of the World to the Death of Moses*. II. *Joshua to Job: Being a Continuation of the Old Testament in Art* (London: Hodder & Stoughton, n.d.), p. 45.

Figure 1: *Jephthah (Judges xi. 35-36)* by Sir J.E. Millais, 1829–96 © The British Museum

her dress is made of a rich fabric and is long and draped. Her hands are clasped to her bosom. A group of six females have or are exiting to the right through a curtained area. They seem to be supportive of each other in their sadness. With one exception, their hair is covered with a scarf or tiara-like piece. Their long dresses are made of beautiful fabrics. The tallest of them looks back over her right shoulder in Jephthah's direction. Peering around the opened curtain is a bearded man. Is he just returning or entering? On the rug near Jephthah's shield is a large scimitar. The left side of this picture is in darkness as is the area behind Jephthah. The young person on the far left turns his head back to the center of the scene, directing the viewer's eyes inward; three women on the right side form closure as they look into the picture and will exit from right to left through the curtain.

2. *Theme Two: Jephthah's Daughter With her Companions on the Mountain* (figure 2).

Ten female figures are either seated or standing on a hillock in this somber painting.[22] The focus is on Jephthah's daughter in the center. Her friends are in groups of two or three as they lounge around her in a rude-shaped circle. She is the only one whose eyes look skyward into the distance. Three figures have their heads cast down. Two look away from the group. One (to the left of center) looks down at an aeolian harp which she holds. One figure seated to her right seems to touch the sleeve of Jephthah's daughter as she gazes up at her. Each is dressed in voluminous clothing and shawl-like head coverings. The dark fabric of their attire is beautifully and minutely textured. The cloth seems to become part of the hilly landscape upon which they sit. Jephthah's daughter wears a scoop-necked blouse with an intricate design around the collar. Sunlight shines on the beautiful but pensive faces of the companions. Despite their lamenting posture, there is an uplift to the scene because of the illumination on the upper torso of each of the two topmost figures. The figure on the top right may be holding a tambourine. In the left foreground is a piece of fabric on which are two upright jugs and an overturned jug. A basket of food is alongside this fabric. There may be a town in the left background.

22. Sparrow, *The Old Testament in Art*, p. 46.

Figure 2: *Jephthah's Daughter: The Days of Mourning* by Henry O'Neil, 1817–80 © The British Museum

3. *Theme Three: The Sacrifice of Jephthah's Daughter* (figure 3).
This is the only indoor scene found with this theme.[23] The setting is a church-like structure. A high vaulted ceiling has beautifully finished beams forming an arch. Seen left to right are Jephthah, his daughter in the absolute center, and a burning pyre on the right. Both are under the arch in the foreground. Where the beams intersect overhead, they form a central circle akin to a light fixture. This imaginary light would shine directly on to the daughter as she is being murdered/sacrificed. How disturbing it is to consider the light as symbolic of God witnessing the fulfillment of Jephthah's vow!

In other pictures Jephthah wielded a scimitar-like death weapon. The kneeling daughter was either in front of a post that vaguely resembled a cross or on a box suggestive of a coffin. In the present scene the clean-shaven Jephthah, clad in intricately designed warrior garb, holds a long, pointed sword aloft with both hands. His armored helmet lies in the left foreground near his right foot, and his scabbard is against his left leg. His pre-adolescent daughter kneels in the usual supplicant's position. Her long hair cascades down her back. She wears a long-sleeved dress that seems to have a long train, against the edge of which rests a sharp pointed spur jutting out of Jephthah's long pointed shoe. While his right foot bears his weight as it is pointed away from his daughter, and his left foot is extended behind her, he is balanced as his body will rotate forward and around in order to kill her. The sphere of action starts just to the right side of center above her head and will travel around to the left, into the immediate foreground, and back into the center where her neck is fully exposed. Leading into the background is the nave. Free standing near the far wall is a draped table or box resting on a low platform, on top of which are two tablets containing unreadable words. Could they be reminiscent of the tablets brought down from Mt Sinai by Moses? As these tablets are examined, it will be noted that Jephthah's raised sword cuts them in half vertically. It is fascinating to ponder whether the 'Thou shall not murder' commandment is effected by the weapon! In light of the backdrop, there are two ways to interpret this picture. First, sacrifices were brought to the Holy Temple in Jerusalem; therefore, this setting is appropriate (although horrific)! Secondly, the idea of sacrificing a person is anathema to any standard of human decency —how much more so within the confines of a religious place—a sanctuary!

---

23. *The Illustrated Bartsch*, LXXXVII, part viii, p. 298. The image reproduced here is included with permission of the British Museum.

Figure 3: *Jephthah Sacrifices his Daughter. Anonymous. 1491.*
Stephan Fridolin. Der Schatzbehalter (Treasure Chest), Nuremberg.
Woodcut. Printed by Anton Koberger
© The British Museum

It is not clear why there are two methods of murder/sacrifice in this scene, namely, the sword and the pyre. Perhaps the daughter's dead body will be offered up as a sacrifice after she has been murdered. Flames move heavenward from the lit pyre. It would be in keeping with the *peshat* to have her offered up as a burnt sacrifice.

The Sacrifice of Jephthah's Daughter (figure 4).
This highly dramatic out of doors scene, depicting a public gathering, will be described from left to right. Two women are seated in the left foreground, one looking in fright at Jephthah and his daughter, the other crouching with her head down on the first woman's knee. Four men on the left are seen from bottom to top of the painting. The lowest one, seated on a chair, gazes at the center action. In front of him is a large, round, flat object. The second is turned away, but his left arm is outstretched back to the center causing the viewer's eye to sense tension of motion. A third points to a book he holds in his hand and may be trying to speak to the center protagonists. A fourth man holds a lit torch in his right hand and glances at the book of the man just below him, and is partially hidden by a long ornate pole which might have a flag on it. Between the third and fourth men is a female whose face only is visible as she stares at Jephthah and his daughter. Jephthah and his daughter are in the center of the painting both longitudinally and latitudinally. Sprawled on a flight of steps outside of a columned, heavily draped entryway of what might be a temple, they are surrounded by men and women who add a sense of agitation and terror to the scene. Some look directly at him and his daughter while others avert their heads. A dog stands on the lowest step in the center foreground. Jephthah, dressed regally in a cape and decorated blouse-like shirt, is seated. His right arm is extended, his left hand rests at his daughter's neck. Under his right hand (and under the book) is a small pitcher filled with fire. This vessel rests on an elaborate pedestal. The daughter, in a dress covered by a cape with a long train, kneels at his feet on a cushion that has a tassel on the visible corner, her head bowed and left arm against his cape. She is the picture of either sadness or tranquility. Jephthah's head is raised as he looks to the right, where he sees an imposing figure looking skyward. Richly attired, draped in a cape and wearing what might be military garb, this man has arresting looking plumage in his helmet. He is presenting a weapon (perhaps a knife or short spear) to Jephthah. While the artist's focal point is the two central figures—Jephthah and his daughter—the man just described is a secondary focal point. Behind him in the background is a large, imposing, arched architectural structure. Just behind his

Figure 4: *The Sacrifice of Jephthah's Daughter* (oil on canvas)
Giovanni Battista Pittoni (1687–1767), painted in 1732–33
Southhampton City Art Gallery, Hampshire UK/Bridgeman Art Library

outstretched arm are three unclear looking faces of onlookers to the scene. In the foreground, below the helmeted man, is a figure who could be either a male or female. It may be a witch with fringes on the shawl of its garb. This person holds up the lid of a cauldron, resting on a tripod from which fire is emanating, peering at the flames. A long chain hangs from the cauldron. Alongside the cauldron is the sandalled foot and leg of a figure whose head is hidden off to the right. Up the steps, on the left, above where Jephthah sits, is what might be an altar surrounded by heavy draped fabric. On the top step are two pitchers.

While Jephthah's community surrounds him, no one other than the standing figure has any obvious rapport or connection with him and his daughter. This is in keeping with the *peshat,* where no mention is made of the people with whom Jephthah lives. However, one is still aghast to realize that Pittoni's interpretation of the daughter's sacrifice clearly indicates that the community bears silent witness to the murder. This is apparent also because of the two sets of fire.

Jephthah's Daughter: The Sacrifice by Charles Le Brun, French School, 1619–90 (figure 5).

Figure 5: *Jephthah's Daughter: The Sacrifice*
by Charles Le Brun, French School, 1619–90
© The British Museum

This painting[24] has a circular shape which helps contain the action and makes the viewer's eye keep moving toward the center. The five figures in it are, from left to right: two females, Jephthah and his daughter, and another woman. While Jephthah is the commanding figure standing masterfully in the center, light focuses on his daughter who semi-reclines at his feet. He is dressed in dark garb, with a lighter colored cape draped over his back and shoulders. Holding his cape with his left hand, his right hand grasps a dagger. His right knee rests against, or is next to, his daughter's lower back. His eyes stare skyward.

The semi-nude, barefoot, beautiful daughter lies on her left side, her draped clothing allowing a partial view of her left breast. She is not a pre-adolescent, as she seems elsewhere. Her eyes are cast downward. It is difficult to ascertain what her emotions are: pensive? sad? accepting? In front of her a companion looks at her, holding a circular object on her knee (perhaps a tray or plate). She looks directly at Jephthah's daughter and I get the sense that she wants to speak to her. Two other females are in front of many spears that stick up in a line across the mid-ground of the picture. The leftmost female holds her head in her hand, thereby not looking at what is to transpire. The inner-placed female peers from alongside Jephthah to see what is going to occur. Next to the two females is a warrior on a horse. He may be holding a furled banner. A tree laden with leaves framing the picture's left side, as well as cloud formations, help keep the viewer's eye coming back to Jephthah. At his shoulder level to the left there is an urn emitting smoke which covers the entire top portion of the painting in ominous fashion. The urn rests on a wall.

Once again, this painting indicates that the daughter will be offered as a burnt sacrifice, although Jephthah does not hold any weapon nor is any visible. Additionally, the witnesses, while appearing curious, are passive and not protesting about what is to occur. Are they powerless? Have they made their peace with the daughter's fate while they were away together for two months? Has the daughter acquiesced entirely and begged the companions not to interfere? Is there a sense of voyeurism on their part and, therefore, they are spectators? Have they been asked by their friend simply to be present so that their telling of her death would be more vivid and revealing during the time they would yearly go to mourn for her?

---

24. Sparrow, *The Old Testament in Art*, p. 45. A subtitle for this image is 'Jephthah's Daughter: The Sacrifice from the Original Picture After a Photograph by G. Brogi'.

E. *Observations*

Theme 1. Jephthah's Return

In each of the scenes showing Jephthah's return from battle, with the exception of Doré's etching, every picture has two parts: the daughter leads a group of females forward to greet the returning Jephthah and his warriors; and the victorious Jephthah leading his warriors. (The Doré image portrays the daughter and her friends only.) The artists have conveyed a sense of sadness or anguish on the companions' faces. The out-of-doors setting with a cloudy sky reinforces the somber mood. However, none of the works shows the females actually sobbing; no tear-streaked faces are drawn. Rather than overtly emoting, the women seem meditative, perhaps supportive of Jephthah's daughter.

The Millais image is a variation of this theme, as it takes place indoors. One could speculate that the out-of-doors scene had already taken place, that the daughter and father are well aware of the implications of her having greeted him, and that she is in the role of comforter here as she holds him protectively.

In the early drawings, the dominant feeling is of a triumphant man returning from battle with no signs of the daughter's joy or Jephthah's anguish. Only in later centuries, as the scene is presented in the medium of painting, do we begin to see the emotion on his face. Finally, in the work by Millais, we observe a devastated Jephthah being comforted by his daughter. In terms of the theme of Jephthah's return, perhaps the artwork could have addressed more poignantly this powerfully passionate scene from the viewpoint of the daughter, as she learned about her father's vow.

A variety of musical instruments is played in the different art works: tambourines, harps, and other percussion instruments. The *peshat* reads תֻפִּים (v. 34), interpreted as 'timbrel(s)', drums or tambourines. In the images, Jephthah's daughter plays different instruments, for example a hand-held harp, bongo drums or a violin. Regarding the dances (מְחֹלוֹת), only the anonymous woodcut and the Doré engraving present the uplifting movement that accompanies the playing of the musical instrument. The other images rather show women standing still as they help greet the returning Jephthah. Is it the more simplistic drawings that show motion, because of the medium? Or did the artists not wish to focus here on the *peshat*?

Theme 2: Jephthah's Daughter and her Friends

The artistic renderings of this theme are in concert with the *peshat* in depicting the daughter and her companions on the mountaintop. There are no references to rabbinic lore (the daughter goes to the mountain to meet the Sanhedrin). Further, keeping *Pseudo-Philo's* exegetical comments in mind, the mountains are stark and there are no animals. The trees and animals in his remarks are not seen weeping and lamenting about her fate.

The question of whether Jephthah's daughter had a mother is pertinent at this point. Following the *peshat* and the majority of interpreters, the images do not, in any of the three themes, show the presence of a woman who might be the mother. Only *Pseudo-Philo* includes a vivid portrait of a mother. The focus of the mountaintop scene is strictly on Jephthah's daughter and her friends. No work has indicated that she had a theophany through the symbolism of an angel, or by a radiant sun with long beams, or by a halo.

Theme 3: The Sacrifice

Place of sacrifice. The *peshat* does not say where or in front of whom Jephthah did to his daughter as he had vowed. The art work demonstrates breadth of exegesis regarding this verse (v. 39). In some images he appears alone with her; other paintings depict numerous witnesses to what he is about to do. The scenes are out of doors except in Fridolin's work. Several works have a religious tone even when there is no church building. The rabbinic *Tanna debe Eliyyahu* has an altar upon which the daughter is to be sacrificed. Variations of this exegetical comment are seen in several drawings.

Method of sacrifice. A scimitar or spear-like weapon appears in some drawings, a flame for a pyre in other images. In every artwork, the daughter will be sacrificed. No alternate method of effectuating Jephthah's vow is indicated. This is in keeping with the majority of Jewish exegetical comments. No picture shows her in solitary confinement as an alternate outcome of the narrative.

The position of Jephthah's daughter. In the older images she is seen as a young female. Only in one does she have a developed woman's figure.

The response of Jephthah's daughter. Earlier drawings portray her in a supplicating position. It is unclear if she is beseeching her father not to murder her or praying to God. According to rabbinic interpretation, she might be either praying to God that she is worthy to be sacrificed or pleading with her father, citing scriptural proof texts that indicate that he should *not* be sacrificing her.

The response of the community. The scenes showing a public gathering indicate no direct interference from the onlookers. Some facial expressions depict horror or shock, but no motion or commotion attempts to stop Jephthah from carrying out his vow. Only in one painting (by Pittoni) is a secondary figure engaged in action with Jephthah, but it is unclear what he is doing: is he trying to thwart Jephthah or is he abetting him? In this same image, one cannot help but wonder what is written in the open book held near Jephthah's arm. Is someone citing biblical prooftexts and admonishing Jephthah not to murder his daughter? Could this man be symbolic of Phineas the High Priest (see rabbinic literature) who has finally stepped forward to save a child's life?

F. *Conclusion*

Emerging from the commentaries was an imbalance and unfairness in the study of the two protagonists. In terms of apologetics, attention was primarily riveted on Jephthah. However, upon further scrutiny of this episode's seven verses, the text seems to focus on the daughter's actions and discourse. She was both active and reactive. Many commentaries avowed that she was respectful toward her father in insisting he fulfill his vow and insightful in comprehending that he must honor his pledge, since God had already made him victorious. In other exegetical comments she challenged her father, pleading that he not take her life.

With the information provided in the biblical verses, more interpretation should have been forthcoming about Jephthah's daughter. Perhaps the challenge of biased interpretation could be levied at later exegetes for their failure to consider her as an independent female with emotions and strengths. As this was valid for rabbinic exegesis, so too was it evident in the art works.

Exegetes pointed with clarity at a heinous error charged to the father, a judge, and to a high priest. According to the targumim and midrashim, the daughter was a victim of the arrogance and obdurateness of these two men. I think that this interpretation appears only in Pittoni's image.

The silent people in this story are missing in the rabbinic exegetical works but do appear in art. Surely in the art works, where the community bears witness to the daughter's death, no sense of communal protest prevents Jephthah from murdering her. Where was Jephthah's wife during the dialogue between Jephthah and his daughter? Why did she not suggest an alternate solution to the fulfillment of the vow? Why did the young girl not seek compassion from her? Similar questions should be posed regarding the returning warriors and all the people in the community. Did no one raise a voice to help Jephthah's daughter? Did the people unanimously accept the execution of the vow without trying to hinder Jephthah from performing the sacrifice? What could the community have done during the time Jephthah's daughter was away with her friends to convince Jephthah that he had alternatives? This story is a traumatic one. Perhaps there was wisdom in the daughter's being unnamed, thereby making identification with her experience one step removed from reality.

Art images that tell the narrative of Jephthah's daughter adhere closely to the scriptural verses. In the portrayal of the two protagonists and the thematic material, setting and mood, the artwork mirrors the text and only occasionally fills in the Bible's lacuna. In themes one and two some deviation is found from the text; theme three allows for more diversity in the representation of the murder weapon and the setting. When contrary opinion is evident in rabbinic interpretation regarding the daughter's fate, it is missing in the art works. Even in later paintings which post-date Radak and Abravanel, each work presents her being sacrificed by her father, that is, she losing her life by his hands. It would therefore seem that the artists were not familiar with targumic or midrashic comments, that they did not know much about rabbinic interpretations. Their focus was more *peshat*-oriented. Yet one might have hoped that the emotions missing in the biblical text would be graphically portrayed by artists. This is so in the later centuries as we move from drawings to prints and etchings and, certainly, to paintings. However, the omission of facial expressions (of joy or anguish) even in the earlier works detracts from the depth of feeling which could be communicated through art. It is as if the biblical gaps are repeated by the artist's brush.

APPENDIX

This Appendix will list (1) the name of the image and its creator, (2) the source book where it can be seen, and (3) selected museums or collections housing the image.[25] (Where this final information is not available, it will be so indicated.)

Theme One: Jephthah's Return

A. 1. *The Pamplona Bible.*

2. This illustration is found in François Bucher, *The Pamplona Bibles: A Facsimile Compiled from Two Picture Bibles with Martyrologies Commissioned by K. Sancho el Fuerte of Navarra (1194–1234). Amiens Manuscript Latin 108 and Harburg MS 1, 2 lat. 4^, 15*, I-II (New Haven: Yale University Press, 1970), pl. 177.

3. Harburg F87R.

B. 1. Old Testament Illustration. Psalter. French artist. c. 1250.

2. Sydney C. Cockerell, *Old Testament Miniatures: A Medieval Picture Book with 283 Paintings From the Creation to the Story of David* (New York: George Braziller, 1969), p. 77.

3. Pierpont Morgan Library. Codex 638.

C. 1. Bible. Lower Saxon, Cologne. Heinrich Quentell, c. 1478.

2. *The Illustrated Bartsch (TIB)* (gen. ed. Walter L. Strauss; New York: Abaris Books, 1978–92), LXXXII, part ii, p. 57.

3. Berlin Staatsbibliothek; British Museum, London; New York Public Library, Rare Book Division, New York City; John H. Scheide Library, Princeton, New Jersey.

D. 1. German miniature.

2. Marcel Brion, *The Bible in Art: Miniatures, Paintings, Drawings and Sculptures Inspired by the Old Testament* (London: Phaidon Press, 1956), illustration #142.

3. Staatsbibliothek, Munich.

E. 1. Stephan Fridolin. 'Jephthah Returns After Battle and Is Greeted by His Daughter'. Der Schatzbehalter (Treasure Chest), Nuremberg. Anton Koberger. 1491.

2. *TIB*, LXXXVII, part viii, p. 297; M. Louis Polain, *Catalogue des livres imprimés au quinzième siècle des bibliothèques de Belgique* (4 vols.; Brussels, 1932).

3. Dresden Kupferstichkabinett; Boston Public Library, Boston; Columbia University, Plimpton Library, NYC; Free Library of Philadelphia, PA; Harvard College Library, Houghton Library, Cambridge, MA.

F. 1. Jephthah and His Daughter. Anonymous. Biblia, German. Strasbourg. Johann (Reinhard) Grüninger. La Bible de Jean Grüninger, 1485.

2. *TIB*, LXXXV, part vi, p. 107.

3. Nuremberg Germanisches Nationalmuseum; The Public Library of Cincinnati and Hamilton County, Cincinnati, Ohio; Union Theological Seminary, NYC.

25. My gratitude is expressed to the following individuals who have helped gather information regarding the location of the images: Marilyn Berger, Head Librarian, Blackader-Lauterman Art Library, McGill University, Montreal (Canada); Yehudit Zenner, Media Dept, University of Haifa (Israel); and Elliot M. Kramer.

G. 1. Jephthah and His Daughter. Jost Amman from Opera Josephi. Woodcut.

2. *TIB*, XX, part ii, p. 757.

3. British Library, London, England.

H. 1. Jephthah and His Daughter (Judges 11), Virgil Solis. From *Biblische Figuren*. Woodcut. Wolfenbüttel. Nuremberg.

2. *TIB*, XIX, part i, p. 303.

3. Herzog August Bibliothek, *Wolfenbüttel* (Monogram VS; A.1.40, Ubisch 40.)

I. 1. Jephthah and His Daughter (Judges 11). Tobias Stimmer. From the *Neue Kunstliche Figuren biblischer Historien*.

2. *TIB*, XIX, part ii, p. 172.

3. Universitätsbibliothek, Basel.

J. 1. Japhthah's Return. Betsy B. Lathrop. Watercolor on Silk. 1812.

2. Lipman and Alice Winchester, *The Flowering of American Folk Art 1776–1876* (New York: Viking, 1974), p. 78. This is a 'watercolor on silk, 22 x $25\frac{3}{4}$', 1812, New England, probably Massachusetts. Signed, dated.

3. Abby Aldrich Rockefeller Folk Art Collection, Williamsburg, Virginia.

K. 1. Jephthah's Daughter Coming to Meet Her Father. Gustave Doré.

2. *The Doré Bible Illustrations: 241 Illustrations by Gustave Doré* (intro. Millicent Rose; New York: Dover Publications, 1974), p. 60. Also found in *The Doré Bible Gallery Containing One Hundred Superb Illustrations and a Page of Explanatory Letter-Press Facing Each: Illustrated by Gustave Doré* (Philadelphia: Henry Altemus, 1890), pl. 23.

3. No information available.

L. 1. Jephthah's Daughter. Artist Unknown. Woodcut.

2. Cynthia Pearl Maus, *The Old Testament and the Fine Arts: An Anthology of Pictures, Poetry, Music, and Stories Covering the Old Testament* (New York: Harper & Brothers, 1954), p. 233.

3. No information available.

M. 1. Jefte de Ritorno dalla Battaglia è Salutato dalla Figlia. Gian Antonio Pellegrine (1675–1741).

2. Pietro Zampetti. *Dal Ricci al Tiepolo: I Pittori di figura del Setticento a Venezia. Catalog /della Mostra* (Venezia: Alfieri, Edizioni D'Arte, 1969), p. 67. Also found in *Burlington Magazine* 102 (1960), p. 78.

3. London: Collection Denis Mahon.

Theme Two: Jephthah's Daughter With her Companions on the Mountain

A. 1. Jephthah's daughter laments with her companions in the mountains.

2. Cockerell, *Old Testament Miniatures*, p. 77. An explanation accompanying this drawing reads: 'A conventional mountain with small trees on R. Jephthah's daughter moves from L in an attitude of grief, followed by seven lamenting virgins' (p. 76).

3. Pierpont Morgan Library, Codex 638.

B. 1. The Daughters of Israel Lamenting the Daughter of Jephthah. Gustave Doré.

2. *Bible Gallery*, pl. 24.

3. No information available.

Theme Three: The Sacrifice of Jephthah's Daughter

A. 1. Jephte's daughter is isolated. Judg.11.39. *Pamplona Bible*.

2. Bucher, plate 178.

3. Harburg F87V.

B. 1. The Sacrifice of Jephthah's Daughter. Anonymous. Spiegel Menschlicher Behaltnis (Mirror of Human Salvation), Augsburg. Anton Sorg. 1476.

2. *TIB*, LXXXI, part ii, p. 90.

3. Munich Bayerische Staatsbibliothek; Vienna Nationalbibliothek; The Newberry Library, Chicago, IL.

C. 1. The Sacrifice of the Daughter of Jephthah. Anonymous. 1476. Speculum Humanae Salvatonis (Mirror of Human Salvation), German, Basel. Bernhard Richel.

2. *TIB*, LXXXI, part ii, p. 29.

3. Berlin Kupferstichkabinett; Pierpont Morgan Library, NYC; Schr 5274. Wilhelm Ludwig Schreiber, *Un catalogue des incunables à figures imprimés en Allemagne, en Suisse, en Autriche-Hongre, et Scandanavie* (two parts; Leipzig, 1910–11) [i.e. vol. 5 of his *Manuel de l'amateur de la gravure sur bois et sur metal au XVe siècle*.

D. 1. The Sacrifice of the Daughter of Jephthah. 1481. Spiegel Menschlicher Behaltnis (Mirror of Human Salvation), Speyer. Peter Drach.

2. *TIB*, LXXXIII, part iv, p. 22.

3. Munich Bayerische Staatsbibliothek; Metropolitan Museum of Art, Department of Prints, NYC, Pierpont Morgan Library (H14935), NYC.

E. 1. Jephthah sacrifices his daughter according to his vow.

2. Cockerell, *Old Testament Miniatures*, p. 77.

3. Pierpont Morgan Library. Codex 638.

DELILAH: A SUITABLE CASE FOR (FEMINIST) TREATMENT?

Carol Smith

Introduction

Delilah is a woman whose name has entered the communal consciousness. People who have not heard of Abishag, or Michal, or Tamar, have heard of Delilah. Not only have they heard of her, they believe they know the type of woman she was. *Chambers' Dictionary* has this entry under 'Delilah': 'the Philistine woman who befooled Samson: a courtesan: a temptress: an alluring object'.[1] Delilah appears because she tempted Samson, 'befooled' him, made a fool of him. Elizabeth Wurtzel writes: 'Delilah's centuries-old superstardom and sex-symbol status has been accorded only because she brought this strong man down'.[2] Samson is, of course, the strong man. Indeed, Chambers' Dictionary has an entry for him also. It reads: 'an abnormally strong man (from the Hebrew champion of Judges xiii-xvi)'.[3] There are no dictionary entries for David, or for Elijah or Isaiah; Abraham is mentioned without reference to the biblical character. Samson appears because of his strength. Delilah appears because of her relationship to Samson, and her name is given as another word for a woman who tempts, who allures, who is sexual. Delilah continues to hold an allure. Samson was, apparently, fascinated by her. Scholars still are. Wurtzel admits in her book that 'bad girls', particularly bad girls who are bad in sexual ways, usually suffer for it, and yet she describes her fascination with the character Delilah: 'From the time I first learned about Delilah when I was ten or eleven years old in elementary school, I wanted to know more'.[4] She notes, 'Delilah to me was a sign of life', '[s]he was sexy and wild and got her way, even if it

---

1. *Chambers 20th Century Dictionary* (ed. E.M. Kirkpatrick; Edinburgh: W. & R. Chambers, new edn, 1983), p. 329.
2. Elizabeth Wurtzel, *Bitch: In Praise of Difficult Women* (London: Quartet Books; New York: Doubleday, 1998), p. 45.
3. *Chambers 20th Century Dictionary*, p. 1144.
4. Wurtzel, *Bitch*, p. 41.

did all come crashing down on her head in the end'.[5] Delilah continues to be a focus for speculation. Because she has been so much discussed and analysed, she provides an ideal starting point for discussions of methods of biblical interpretation, particularly methods of feminist biblical interpretation.

Why Does Delilah Fascinate?

So why does Delilah fascinate? Primarily because of the nature of the story. It has been observed that:[6]

> The most important qualities of this type of woman are beauty, sensuousness, intelligence, self-assurance, cunning, and persistence. All these qualities are used to bring about the fall of a man previously thought to be infallible and unbeatable. The basic scheme pits feminine wiles against masculine strength, clever stratagems against physical prowess, words versus mute action.

In fact,[7]

> the story contains many motifs capable of development—patriotism versus individualism, man's strength versus woman's cunning, religious vocation versus sensuous entanglement.

She also fascinates, I think, because there are certain unanswerable questions about Delilah, which provide food for speculation. For example, was she wife or harlot? It is often assumed that Delilah was a prostitute, but the text nowhere states that she was (although this assumption itself says something about interpreters). What does the name 'Delilah' really mean? Why is the biblical text ambiguous about whether she is a Philistine or an Israelite? Exum rightly points out[8] that we cannot simply assume (as so many commentators do) that the woman is a Philistine. Delilah has a Hebrew name. From where does she originate? She lives on the boundary between Israelite and Philistine territory. The text presents at least the possibility that Delilah is an Israelite. Why does she simply fade out of the narrative after Samson has been captured? Each of these questions is open to more than one answer. There is an ambiguity about Delilah in the many silences regarding her in the biblical text. But the ambiguity may be deliberate,

5.   Wurtzel, *Bitch*, pp. 44 and 45.
6.   D. Sölle, J.H. Kirchberger and H. Haag, *Great Women of the Bible in Art and Literature* (trans. J.H. Kirchberger; Grand Rapids, MI: Eerdmans, 1993), p. 138.
7.   Sölle, Kirchberger and Haag, *Great Women of the Bible*, p. 141.
8.   J.C. Exum, 'Samson's Women', in *idem, Fragmented Women: Feminist (Sub)versions of Biblical Narratives* (JSOTSup, 163; Sheffield: JSOT Press, 1993), pp. 61-93 (69).

reflecting the ambiguity of the woman herself, her behaviour, her relationships, her position in society. For these reasons, she is both discussed and pointedly not discussed, by both traditional and feminist biblical scholars.

One can see why Delilah has been described as stereotypical. Whether one regards her positively or negatively, her behaviour is not unusual. Her whole story conforms to a pattern. Wurtzel describes the story of Samson and Delilah as 'the archetypal story of cross-cultural love between members of warring nations: this is Romeo and Juliet... Essentially, the story of Samson and Delilah is one of fatal love, where someone is bound to die'.[9] Feminist commentators have thus been left with a choice: ignore Delilah as a character and concentrate on other biblical women who are more amenable to reinterpretation in a more positive way; or 'rehabilitate' her by emphasizing her strengths and positive qualities; or acknowledge and attempt to explain her more negative traits. The first option—ignoring Delilah—is a tempting one and some feminists have ignored her. This is not simply a matter of avoiding a difficult text because of laziness or incompetence. It is tied up with perceptions of what is the task of feminist biblical scholarship. It could be argued that energies would be better spent on other passages whose reinterpretation could be used for the benefit of women, particularly those who are members of worshipping communities or undertaking academic study. It could also be argued that if the text about Delilah really is extremely negative, focusing further attention upon it runs the risk of reinforcing the androcentric and misogynistic misconceptions about the biblical text that feminist biblical scholars hope to help eradicate. Often, the factors underlying a decision about whether or not to be selective about biblical texts are questions not only about the texts themselves, but about the nature of feminist biblical scholarship, and about feminism itself. Having said this, being selective about texts, for whatever reasons, lays one open to charges of exclusivity, prejudice, scholarly cowardice, or even dishonesty. Feminist interpreters have treated the story in a wide variety of ways. I shall be returning to some of these interpretations of Delilah below.

Why should there be so many different ways of seeing this woman? The answer lies, I think, in the nature of biblical interpretation, and of feminist biblical interpretation. We believed, in the early days, that there ought to be one 'feminist interpretation' of a biblical story. We have learned that this is not the case. In fact, women calling themselves

9. Wurtzel, *Bitch*, p. 41.

'feminists' hold a variety of different viewpoints. Also, women holding what are traditionally believed to be 'feminist' views do not call
themselves 'feminists' at all. When we look at the history of feminist
biblical interpretation, it is possible to see how differing approaches to
the text are possible. The different ways in which feminists have
responded to the story of Delilah reflect some of the developments in
feminist interpretation of the Bible over the last few decades.

The Beginnings of Feminist Interpretation of the Old Testament

Several possible ways of looking at biblical texts have emerged in
feminist writing. They may loosely be described as follows: that the
Bible is not as patriarchal and as negative about women as has sometimes been assumed; that the Bible is indeed patriarchal, but is redeemable, providing its context is taken into account; and that the
Bible is irredeemable and should therefore be disregarded. Obviously,
there are scholars whose work overlaps between one or more of these
categories and various subdivisions within them, but this description
gives an overall picture.

Feminist biblical interpretation began with scholars who were committed to their work and to the Bible, but who found it difficult to
reconcile their feminism with what they believed the Bible to contain.
Phyllis Trible, whose groundbreaking book, *God and the Rhetoric of
Sexuality*, appeared in 1978, writes this in the Foreword to the book:

> I realized that the theology which informed my life was inadequate for
> addressing the concerns of students; nor was it wholly satisfying for me.
> Ironically, the mighty acts of God in history proved wanting, and the
> ensuing years have heightened that deficiency.[10]

She goes on:

> Using feminist hermeneutics, I have tried to recover old treasures and
> discover new ones in the household of faith. Though some of these trea-
> sures are small, they are nonetheless valuable in a tradition that is often
> compelled to live by the remnant.[11]

One more quotation from Trible's 1978 work:

> Among the blessings of this day has been developing interest, in my
> part, in interdisciplinary study. This interest expresses itself in various
> ways throughout the manuscript: literary criticism flavors the text from

---

10. P. Trible, *God and the Rhetoric of Sexuality* (Overtures to Biblical Theology;
Philadelphia: Fortress Press, 1978), p. xv.
11. Trible, *God and the Rhetoric of Sexuality*, p. xvi.

beginning to end; psychoanalytic terminology appears in one section; and existentialism, philosophical hermeneutics, structuralism, and Zen Buddhism figure here and there. Though these idioms are not the language of Zion, I welcome their contributions to my understanding, even as I remember the beneficial presence of Ruth the Moabite in the faith of Israel.[12]

Trible's work came as a breath of fresh air to women struggling to combine their faith and their feminism and others soon followed her lead. Although *God and the Rhetoric of Sexuality* was critiqued and found wanting in some respects,[13] its importance continues to be acknowledged. It showed a new way of looking at biblical texts and Trible's work on Genesis 2–3 opened the door to looking at other texts about women in a new light. However, it soon became apparent that not all the misogyny and androcentrism that has been found in biblical passages relating to women could be put down to inadequate methods of interpretation. It became clear that however full of hope feminists were at the discovery of the work of Trible and others like her, such as Katherine Doob Sakenfeld, with their bringing of texts about women into the foreground and highlighting how much other factors in an androcentric world had influenced their interpretation, it had to be acknowledged that some texts simply could not be reinterpreted positively. Something more was needed and attempts were made to 'redeem' and reclaim such texts. The obvious example of this is Trible's second important book, *Texts of Terror*. In this book, the stories of women are retold. Trible acknowledges that there are 'sad stories' in the Bible: 'Indeed, they are tales of terror with women as victims'.[14] She tells the stories because '[s]torytelling is sufficient unto itself', and '[a]ncient tales of terror speak all too frighteningly of the present'.[15] Other books appeared, such as Carol Meyers' *Discovering Eve*[16] and others looking for overall themes that counteract the effects of individual passages.

12. Trible, *God and the Rhetoric of Sexuality*, pp. xvi-xvii.

13. See, for example, D.J.A. Clines, 'What Does Eve Do to Help? And Other Irredeemably Androcentric Orientations in Genesis 1–3', in D.J.A. Clines, *What Does Eve Do to Help? And Other Readerly Questions to the Old Testament* (JSOTSup, 94; Sheffield: JSOT Press, 1990), pp. 25-48.

14. P. Trible, *Texts of Terror: Literary-Feminist Readings of Biblical Narratives* (Philadelphia: Fortress Press, 1984), p. 1.

15. Trible, *Texts of Terror*, p. xiii.

16. C. Meyers, *Discovering Eve: Ancient Israelite Women in Context* (Oxford: Oxford University Press, 1988).

Trible acknowledges the difficulties of some biblical texts about women when she reviews her position in an article in *Bible Review* entitled 'If the Bible's so Patriarchal, How Come I Love It?'.[17] In this article Trible outlines the problems facing feminist interpreters of the Old Testament:

> The Bible was born and bred in a land of patriarchy; it abounds in male imagery and language. For centuries, interpreters have exploited this androcentrism to articulate theology; to define the church, synagogue and academy; and to instruct human beings, female and male, in who they are, what roles they should play and how they should behave. So harmonious has seemed this association of scripture with sexism, of faith with culture, that few have ever questioned it. Understandably, then, when feminism turns attention to the Bible, it first of all names patriarchy.[18]

Trible continues:

> Evidence abounds for the subordination, inferiority and abuse of women. One has no difficulty in making this case against the Bible; it is the sine qua non of all feminist readings.[19]

> Interpreting the Bible with a feminist hermeneutic does not mean, however, that every text turns out to be non-patriarchal, or at least less so. In some cases, analysis shows how much more patriarchal a passage is. The challenge to redeem Scripture must then be met differently [from my handling of the creation account]... While the establishment prefers to forget its use and abuse of women, feminism wrestles with the meaning of it all. To accord these stories happy endings would be preposterous; yet to succumb to their suffering would be destructive. The demanding task is to retell them on behalf of the victims.[20]

Trible calls such an approach not simply the exposure of misogyny, but 'a dialectic of redemption. *Reinterpretation remembers in order not to repeat. Its memorial calls for repentance*'.[21] The way was opened for new approaches to difficult passages about women, and Trible's *Texts of Terror* was an important contribution to this development.

> If patriarchal exegesis has neglected threatening passages over the centuries, we need not assume that they are all texts of terror demeaning to women. To the contrary, they may be signs of female strength, hints of woman's tradition that redactors could not entirely squelch... The story

17. P. Trible, 'If the Bible's so Patriarchal, How Come I Love It?', *BR* 8.5 (1992), pp. 44-47, 55.

   18. Trible, 'If the Bible's so Patriarchal...', p. 45.

   19. Trible, 'If the Bible's so Patriarchal...', p. 47.

   20. Trible, 'If the Bible's so Patriarchal...', p. 55.

   21. Trible, 'If the Bible's so Patriarchal...', p. 55 (Trible's italics).

> is not yet finished. There are miles to go in exegesis and appropriation. At times, travel is difficult and dangerous. Like Jeremiah, I sense that enemies are around to reproach and denounce.[22]

I have quoted Trible extensively, because her work has been so fundamental and so formative of feminist biblical criticism. We notice several points about her analysis of her position that seem to be almost an agenda for the work that was to follow. First, she clearly comes from within a worshipping tradition and continues to regard the Bible as being 'Scripture' in some sense of the word. Secondly, she sees the task as one that is not yet complete. There is still much work to be done. Thirdly, she emphasizes the importance of interdisciplinary approaches. Lastly, perhaps surprisingly, Trible does not foresee that the task will become easier. Perhaps the unwritten thought there is that some of the 'enemies' of which she speaks will come from within the ranks of feminists themselves.

Feminist Exegesis: A Summary

Trible and her contemporaries were pioneers. Although Trible's work could not have been carried out without her use of the methods of literary criticism, she was trained in traditional ways and used the analytical tools and linguistic skills derived from that training. In fact, there has been a constant interchange between feminist criticism and the wider discipline, and new methods, such as rhetorical criticism, opened the door for feminists to bring their particular perspectives to the Old Testament.

So, what has happened since *God and the Rhetoric of Sexuality*? Many have built on Trible's work, while others have moved far from her starting point. Much of feminist Old Testament scholarship has recently changed direction and it could be argued that, like many other areas within biblical studies, it is becoming separated from its more traditionalist roots. Feminist interpretation of the Old Testament has not grown up in isolation from the rest of biblical studies. Feminist interpretation includes critiques of scholarly methods, including feminist ones. The rise of 'reader response' criticism, and the acknowledgment that a reader's context shapes the ways in which he or she reads a text enabled feminists to point out that even when unacknowledged, the patriarchal agenda was certainly present. It also became clear that the methods that had traditionally been used in academic biblical scholarship did not facilitate feminist readings. What was

---

22. Trible, 'If the Bible's so Patriarchal...', p. 55.

needed were ways of exploring new methods and their implications. However, exploring new methods also has its limitations. As Pamela Milne has pointed out,[23]

> We initially attempted to locate the patriarchy problem in interpretation. But the more work we did, the more evidence we found that pointed to the Bible itself.

One way of dealing with this, Milne suggests, is to focus more on the reader than on the biblical text itself:[24]

> ...every text has gaps or silences and...every author assumes readers bring some knowledge to their reading. Readers actually create new texts by combining their knowledge with what they encounter in the written text. This development in thinking seems to offer a new possibility to feminists who want to salvage the authority of the Bible. The strategy is to relocate meaning away from the text to the reader or the process of reading.

There is, however, a fundamental problem for feminist readers using the argument that their own 'reader response' to a text is a valid one. This is that they also have to allow the validity of other readings, however alien to their own feminist philosophy. Also, the use by Trible and her contemporaries of literary critical methods had as its background a thorough grounding in traditional scholarship. It sometimes seems as if those with no such grounding who simply approach the text and deal with it in a superficial way present a house built on sand rather than one built on rock. The house built on sand is held up by ideology and willpower and if those are undermined, then the whole edifice will fall.

The process of feminist interpretation began by simply reading the Old Testament and rediscovering within it stories of women that had hitherto been neglected. Many biblical stories about women were 'rediscovered' by feminists and the assumptions underlying what had previously been said about them analysed and critiqued. Furthermore, many of these stories were then reinterpreted in the light of feminist insights. Books appeared, with the purpose of showing that many of the negative statements that had previously been made about women of the Bible had their roots in the androcentric world-views of commentators rather than in the biblical text itself. Thus, the positive

23. P.J. Milne, 'No Promised Land: Rejecting the Authority of the Bible', in H. Shanks (ed.), *Feminist Approaches to the Bible* (Washington, DC: Biblical Archaeology Society, 1995), pp. 47-73 (p. 65).

24. Milne, 'No Promised Land', p. 66.

aspects of biblical women were emphasized, such as the leadership of Deborah, independent behaviour by Sarah, and so on.

This process is what led to the questioning of why and how this neglect had come about. This in turn led to a questioning of traditional scholarly method and the validity of its apparent claims to 'objectivity'. Feminists working in other areas had begun to observe the ubiquity of androcentric values and norms and their insidious effects on the lives of women and these insights were utilized by feminist biblical scholars. They began to suggest that texts about women had been misunderstood and that led to an examination of the academic and cultural contexts in which such misunderstanding had occurred. It needs to be reiterated that such an analysis would not have been possible had the feminist scholars concerned not been trained in traditional methods and thus understood the ways in which they were used.

There began to be a reassessment of texts relating to women, whether these were narratives about women, laws pertaining to women, or metaphorical language and feminine imagery. It was perhaps inevitable that some texts should have received more attention than others, particularly at first. Trible's *God and the Rhetoric of Sexuality* has a large section on Genesis 2–3, and this became (and still is) a crucial text for feminist biblical interpreters, because of the use that has been made of it from 2 Timothy onwards. It is no coincidence that Brenner's edited volume, *A Feminist Companion to Genesis*,[25] should have its largest section devoted to the same chapters. More positive portrayals of Old Testament women were set against negative ones. Part of this process involved setting narratives and legal texts in the wider context of the Old Testament and the ancient Near East. This would not have been possible had Old Testament study generally not begun to move away from ever more detailed examinations of linguistic matters and towards a more holistic approach. As already noted, feminist criticism could not have happened without the advent of literary criticism and reader response methods. In my view it also could not have happened without the background of canonical criticism and structuralism. All such methods reflect the belief that although the Old Testament reflects a patriarchal, even misogynistic society, is it redeemable by feminist interpretation and reinterpretation.

25. A. Brenner (ed.), *A Feminist Companion to Genesis* (The Feminist Companion to the Bible, 2; Sheffield: Sheffield Academic Press, 1993).

However, for some feminists this was not enough. Other questions began to be asked. Is the biblical text inherently and irredeemably patriarchal? Linked to this were questions about whether it was possible to free readers from centuries of interpretation. Some decided that there was no possibility of redeeming the biblical text in any way. In fact, the 'text' as we have it, includes the history of its interpretation. And although at first feminist biblical scholars concentrated on interpretation by other biblical scholars, latterly, other scholars, notably J. Cheryl Exum and Alice Bach, following in the footsteps of Mieke Bal and other cultural interpreters, included in 'the history of interpretation' all cultural representations of biblical motifs and characters. As Exum points out in *Plotted, Shot, and Painted*,[26] 'As a woman and a feminist, I have something at stake in the cultural representations of biblical women'. The responses to this varied, according to the context of the person concerned. Some feminists in the Christian tradition decided that the only option was to become post-Christian and discard the Bible altogether. These feminists argued that the Bible was not only irrelevant, it was positively dangerous. Here is Daphne Hampson, writing in 1990:[27]

> Such textual analysis [i.e. feminist interpretation], undertaken with a feminist pair of eyes, is uncovering the depth at which sexism must be seen to be present in the text. It shows to be totally naive claims that the problem of the patriarchal nature of the biblical literature could be solved by for example substituting certain female words for male words, or concentrating on those stories which contain women. The text is the product of a sexist, indeed, misogynist, culture: the presuppositions of a patriarchal world are written into it. Moreover, such texts are the more dangerous in that they affect us at a subconscious level. The fact that the narrator evaluates the story from a patriarchal perspective only compounds the issue. There is, one must conclude, little that can be done. Yet these texts are read as sacred texts.

Milne states:[28]

> There is a significant need for feminist critical analysis of the Bible and its effects on our society, but I doubt we will be perceived as serious feminist people as long as we try to fit the notion of an authoritative sacred canon into a feminist paradigm. The more important task, in my view, is to situate our work more centrally within the ongoing struggle for women's equality.

26. J.C. Exum, *Plotted, Shot, and Painted* (JSOTSup, 215; Gender, Culture, Theory, 3; Sheffield: Sheffield Academic Press, 1996), p. 11.

27. D. Hampson, *Theology and Feminism* (Signposts in Theology; Oxford: Basil Blackwell, 1990), p. 92.

Milne, like Hampson, sees a conflict between being a feminist and seeing the Bible as an 'authoritative' text. Both would, I think, place their commitment to feminist ideals and values above any claims the Bible might have over them. Milne writes:[29]

> A non-confessing feminist discourse, rather than subordinating the feminist perspective, subjects the biblical text and tradition to evaluation from feminist value systems. Feminist biblical scholars who are working in non-confessional contexts might well promote dialogue with other feminists by emphasizing this and by making a greater effort to articulate the feminist goal or purpose [whatever that may be] of their work.

But whereas Hampson advocates disregarding it altogether, Milne suggests that biblical study is essential for the continuing feminist struggle. This view is shared by those, such as Mieke Bal, Cheryl Exum, Alice Bach and others, who approach the Bible as a cultural artefact. They begin from the premise that

> It is not simply a matter of the Bible influencing culture; the influence takes place in both directions. What many people know or think they know about the Bible comes from more familiar representations of biblical texts and themes in the popular culture than from study of the ancient text itself.[30]

While broadly agreeing with this statement, I would wish to add: 'often, but not always', as I think this is a factor that is too frequently overlooked.

This consciousness of the place of the Bible as part of the wider culture and the need for feminism to critique that culture as a whole, has led some feminists to look through their feminist eyeglasses at the Bible in the context of that wider culture. J. Cheryl Exum, in *Plotted, Shot and Painted*, examines the ways in which biblical women such as Delilah and Bathsheba are portrayed by filmmakers; Mieke Bal had already brought the insights and methods of the study of literature to the Bible, in *Murder and Difference*;[31] and Ilona Rashkow has used 'a

---

28.   Milne, 'No Promised Land', p. 70.

29.   P.J. Milne, 'Toward Feminist Companionship: The Future of Biblical Studies and Feminism', in A. Brenner and C. Fontaine (eds.), *A Feminist Companion to Reading the Bible: Approaches, Methods and Strategies* (Sheffield: Sheffield Academic Press, 1997), pp. 39-60 (58).

30.   Exum, *Plotted, Shot, and Painted*, pp. 7-8.

31.   M. Bal, *Murder and Difference: Gender, Genre, and Scholarship on Sisera's Death* (trans. M. Gumpert; Bloomington: Indiana University Press, 1988); see also, M. Bal (ed.), *Anti-Covenant: Counter-Reading Women's Live in the Hebrew Bible* (JSOTSup, 81; Bible and Literature Series, 22; Sheffield: Almond Press, 1989).

feminist-psychoanalytic approach' to some biblical texts in her book, *The Phallacy of Genesis*.[32] However, these new developments and perspectives need themselves to be subject to scrutiny, since they call into question much that has gone before in feminist interpretation of the Old Testament and even, implicitly, the integrity of the scholars engaged in it. As such their work could have powerful implications for the future of feminist Old Testament scholarship.

The approach of scholars such as Bal and Exum acknowledges the Bible's importance in the shaping of Western patriarchal ideology, and studies it precisely because of this importance. Such scholars accept that the Bible is a sacred text for some, but do not take it as such for themselves. This view completes the separation of the Bible from the worshipping community. However, if used on its own, it is ultimately sterile. It is perhaps significant that in her Preface to *Plotted, Shot, and Painted*, Exum thanks Alice Bach 'for saying "it doesn't have to go anywhere"', because, in fact, it could be argued that, ultimately, Exum's work does not 'go anywhere'.[33] Once you have analysed every single biblical text relating to women and every single cultural artefact making reference to those texts, and discovered them to be irredeemably patriarchal, where do you go next? There is also a basic confusion underlying much of the work in this area. It is argued that the underlying text is deeply misogynistic, written by males from a male perspective, and with male readers in mind, and yet there seems to be in much of their work an air of general condemnation of artists, authors and filmmakers for reinforcing such images in their portrayals of biblical women. It should not really surprise us that they do so. Hollywood may be 'larger than life', but the whole point is that it starts from 'life'! In fact, there is something of a parallel in speaking of the Bible. The Old Testament stories are derived from a culture that was in many ways patriarchal and androcentric, and that, in my view, moved over time further and further towards outright misogyny, for various reasons. It would be surprising indeed if the writings of that time did not reflect that wider cultural context, and the knowledge that they do reflect it should give us hope in the signs of redemption that have been found for feminists in the biblical text, since they indicate that if a progression in one direction is possible, it is also possible in the other direction.

---

32. I. Rashkow, *The Phallacy of Genesis: A Feminist-Psychoanalytic Approach* (Literary Currents in Biblical Interpretation; Louisville, KY: Westminster/John Knox, 1993).

33. Exum, *Plotted, Shot, and Painted*, p. 15.

Much useful work has been done by cultural critics such as Bal, Bach and Exum in uncovering the reinforcement of negative images of biblical women in the arts and the media, and one would have assumed that the logical progression from their work would be that there should be a call to a return to the Old Testament so that the record can be put right. If, as so many would claim, the Bible does indeed contain the seeds of its own subversion, might it also be possible that if cultural artefacts reflect not only their cultural context, but also something of the nature of the Bible itself, then cultural artefacts might also contain similar seeds of their own subversion? While works of art, and literature and films have emphasized and reinforced certain aspects of biblical portrayals of women, there are other aspects, of equal importance, that also need to be brought into the foreground. Nevertheless, the whole tenor of the work of Exum, Bach and others is that there is no hope. The more works of art and aspects of popular culture, such as films, are examined, the more misogyny is to be found in them. Bach makes an assumption that the biblical text, like the 'meta-texts' derived from it, is inherently misogynistic and biased against the interests of women, and that it is only with the help of scholars such as herself and others like her that women can be rescued from being victims of this ideological conspiracy. This appears to contain within it a further assumption—that those readers, female or male, who do not perceive this overwhelming and irreparable bias within the biblical texts and the cultural artefacts based upon them, are somehow stupid, ignorant, deluded, or merely the tools of the patriarchal establishment. The problem is that if one believes that the biblical text is riddled with patriarchy, androcentrism and misogyny, then everywhere you look for it in the Bible you will find it. There needs to be a clearer distinction made between the world in which the biblical text took its form and the text itself, even granting that the two are obviously interconnected. The Bible reflects something of the world-view that prevailed at the time it was written, as well as contributing to its construction. It also, obviously, has contributed to the world-view of Western culture and scholars are right to point this out. Nevertheless, there seems to be no recognition of the possibility that 'misogyny' then took different forms from 'misogyny' today. It is assumed that what constitutes 'patriarchy', 'androcentrism', and 'misogyny' is a constant, even though these concepts have only been actively formulated and explored in the twentieth century. Further, the terms 'misogyny', 'androcentrism' and 'patriarchy' are not synonymous and we have not yet explored fully the possibility that the Bible (and its 'metatexts') might be patriarchal and androcentric without necessarily being misogynistic. This is an area that needs more attention.

Exum's stated aim in her book *Plotted, Shot, and Painted* is to 'explore how our culture reads texts and visual images of biblical women'.[34] Competent though it is, there are serious questions to be asked about her work and its relevance to biblical scholarship. Although Exum pays lip service to the fact that '[she is the] main instance of how a reader or viewer responds, since I know my experience best',[35] she gives the distinct impression that she believes her own interpretation of cultural representations of biblical women to be the only valid one. This tendency is increased in the work of others, such as Bach, who has commented: 'A central cause of women bearing the weight of patriarchy is to be found in the biblical portraits of women'.[36] Her book is an attempt to demonstrate the truth of this statement. In fact, there is a serious question in my mind about whether the work of such scholars should be regarded as either biblical scholarship or feminism, even though Bach's work is described by her publisher as 'a shift in the paradigm of biblical study'[37] and Exum's *Plotted, Shot, and Painted* appears in the *Journal for the Study of the Old Testament* Supplement Series. It needs to be asked whether the work of those dealing with 'the tropes and figures of the Bible [that] reside in the collective unconscious of Western culture as well as in the conscious streams of moralizing that drench our popular media'[38] can really be classed as biblical interpretation at all, feminist or otherwise. There is a wider question here about whether there should be boundaries about what can and what cannot be classed as 'biblical interpretation' and what they are. How far does one have to move away from the biblical text for the study that is undertaken, however scholarly, to be regarded as the study of something other than the Bible? There is also a question about whether work that has at its heart a denial of the perceptions and experience of women readers of texts or metatexts can be termed 'feminist', since feminism has at its roots the acknowledgment of the validity of the experiences and perspectives of women. This area also needs to be explored, since, clearly, there are women who would describe themselves as feminists who do

34. Exum, *Plotted, Shot, and Painted*, p. 11.
35. Exum, *Plotted, Shot, and Painted*, p. 11.
36. A. Bach, *Women, Seduction and Betrayal in Biblical Narrative* (Cambridge: Cambridge University Press, 1997), p. 1.
37. Bach, *Women, Seduction and Betrayal*, back cover.
38. Bach, *Women, Seduction and Betrayal*, p. 1.

not see the biblical text as irredeemably androcentric and misogynistic. There are also alternative ways of interpreting many of the cultural artefacts that have been deemed as perpetuating male-centred perceptions of the Bible. Where one cultural critic sees evidence of a (detrimental and oppressive) 'male gaze', another may well see something very different, and even liberating. There is, further, as I have already noted, an inherent inconsistency at the heart of all studies rooted in 'reader response' criticism and postmodernist biblical interpretation. If all readings have equal validity, then overtly patriarchal and misogynistic readings have to be counted as potentially valid, even by feminists, however offensive such readings may appear.

Bach writes:[39]

> A majority of feminist intellectuals have freed themselves from the religious biases first planted in the Garden that continue to teach androcentrism as God's law. But this is not enough to change a culture.

However, there needs to be some clarification here about the task being undertaken. Either the culture is being described and analysed or attempts are being made to change it. There can be no doubt that these two tasks are interrelated, but they are nevertheless distinct, and should be distinguished.

The underlying assumptions about biblical stories and characters and cultural artefacts derived from them (such as films, paintings, etc.) that lie behind the work of some cultural critics, could, if taken to their logical conclusion, have profound implications not only for feminist biblical interpretation of the Bible, but also other methods of interpretation. Such an agenda can have negative consequences in two particularly significant areas: the work of feminist biblical scholars and the status of the Bible for members of worshipping communities. If the Bible *and every subsequent interpretation of it* is, by definition, irredeemably sexist and even misogynistic, any form of feminist biblical scholarship becomes impossible and the work of all feminist scholars to date is called into question as being either naive or deliberately misleading. Further, suggesting that the Bible cannot be regarded as in any way authoritative for any morally upright person calls into question the existence of any community whose mode of existence is tied to the Bible as an authoritative document (however that may be interpreted, and it could include a whole spectrum of worshipping communities from the fundamentalist to the exceedingly liberal).

---

39. Bach, *Women, Seduction, and Betrayal*, p. 2.

Further, while Exum declares, possibly rightly, that even texts *about* women are written by males with a male reader in mind, it is extraordinary that she should imply that not until now has this been realized. Although it may not have been expressed in the same language, it is surely the case that the first female readers to have looked with feminist eyes upon the Bible—going back even beyond Trible to Elizabeth Cady Stanton and her co-workers in the production of *The Woman's Bible*, published in 1895—were doing just that: reading with women's eyes, and gradually becoming aware of the implications of what they were reading. And as they read and interpreted what they read, and critiqued the tradition of interpretation that had been handed down to them, they began the process of undermining those layers that had accrued over the centuries. In fact, there is a good pedigree for such an approach. Surely, the whole concept of midrash is that the tradition is there to be debated and explored.

Nevertheless, rather than advocating a constructive return to the text, which is where feminist biblical interpretation began, and which seems a sensible place for all biblical scholarship to begin, many scholars seem to be conveying the distinct impression that they have already made up their minds that the text is irredeemable. Rather than discard the Bible, as Hampson does, they continually pick over it, looking for more and more examples of patriarchal bias and misogyny. They will never see a redeeming feature and discount all efforts to demonstrate that they exist, or can exist. Such an approach can be helpful as a contribution to a wider engagement with biblical texts, particularly a wider feminist engagement. It has little value as a method used in isolation.

Feminist Interpretation of Delilah

One of the first tasks undertaken by feminist biblical scholars was the rediscovery of biblical women. The trouble is, I think, that feminists were not sure whether they wanted to rediscover Delilah, that mixture of strength and weakness; a woman using all those 'feminine' weapons we most deplore—tears, nagging, sexual attraction—and yet achieving her aims by doing it. It has to be admitted that Delilah's behaviour brought her financial independence, surely something to be applauded by feminists! But we are made uncomfortable by Delilah using the limited power that she has, particularly her sexual power, so effectively, and doing so in ways that are stereotypical and seen as negative according to feminist 'orthodoxy'. In fact, Delilah *is* a 'type', one of 'a line of noteworthy seductresses frequently assigned to a strong hero by legends and folktales'.[40] She represents a particular view of women that has been castigated by the patriarchal establishment and feminists alike and that sits uneasily in a feminist context. Post-feminists might be much more comfortable with Delilah's behaviour!

So what methods are available for feminists to use in dealing with the story of Delilah? Is it possible to say that the Bible is not as negative and patriarchal about Delilah as has sometimes been assumed? Those who have taken this route believe so. They are in effect saying that while at first glance it may seem that Judges 16 is about a strong man, if the story is carefully read, it can be seen that it is also about a strong woman. One suggestion is that[41]

> It is possible that the original Samson legend was invented by the Philistines, for whom Delilah thus becomes a patriotic heroine.

Lillian Klein has mad a similar point, suggesting that from a Philistine point of view (and Klein assumes that Delilah is a Philistine), she may be seen as 'a resourceful woman, possibly a heroine to her own people', in spite of perpetrating 'an age-old and repugnant ruse: using a man's love to bring him down'. [42] Klein also comments,[43] 'Delilah cannot be faulted for serving her people'. Thus, even if one accepts that the biblical writer has a negative perception of Delilah, it is still possible to redeem her to some extent by emphasizing some of her positive qualities. Another method feminist interpreters have used when considering biblical women has been seeing stories from the point of view of a woman participant or observer. Thus, it can be argued that seen from the perspective of a Philistine woman, Delilah can be seen as an example of a woman who is patriotic and shows initiative. It may well be the case that from the biblical writer's point of view, Delilah is one of the women 'who endanger the society in which they live to the point of physical destruction',[44] but seen from another perspective she is a positive model of female independence, imagination and self-sufficiency.

40. Sölle, Kirchberger and Haag, *Great Women of the Bible*, p. 138.

41. Sölle, Kirchberger and Haag, *Great Women of the Bible*, p. 141.

42. L.R. Klein, 'The Book of Judges: Paradigm and Deviation in Images of Women', in A. Brenner (ed.), *A Feminist Companion to Judges* (The Feminist Companion to the Bible, 4; Sheffield: JSOT Press, 1993), p. 66.

43. Klein, 'The Book of Judges', p. 65.

44. A. Brenner, *The Israelite Woman: Social Role and Literary Type in Biblical Narrative* (Sheffield: JSOT Press, 1985), p. 113.

Danna Nolan Fewell is one of those who believes that Delilah has been given a bad press. She comments:[45]

> Delilah is rarely examined in her own right. Because Samson is often labelled a hero, Delilah is cast in the role of a villain who brings about the downfall of God's chosen. Delilah, however, is more than an (un?)-supporting actress. In this part of the story, the spotlight is hers. Of all the women in Samson's story, she alone is named. Once introduced, she initiates the action. It is her desire that drives the plot; Samson is merely a respondent. The woman is the focus of the reader's attention.
>   Delilah's identity is not bound to any man. Introduced simply by name, she is a woman who takes care of herself. She conducts her love affair with Samson and her business affairs with the lords of the Philistines without any father, brother, or husband acting as mediator...
> Delilah, a woman without father, brother, or husband to support her, secures for herself financial stability.

Others have also noted Delilah's independence. Lillian Klein notes[46] that 'Delilah is presented as an unusually independent woman who engages in direct commercial enterprises with men and uses her sexuality to tangible advantage'. However, in Klein's view[47] this is used by the biblical writer in a negative way, since because 'Delilah, the woman [Samson] loves, betrays him for the lowest of purposes: a price. To the Israelite reader, Delilah is depicted as worse than a prostitute'. In fact, she is 'the female climax in Judges' cyclical sequence of flawed characters'. Nevertheless, it does need to be said that while independence, and particularly financial independence, is desirable for twentieth-century women, this was not necessarily the case in ancient Israel. A woman without male support may well have been seen as an object for pity rather than congratulation.

Delilah appears to have been an independent woman;[48] and to have had a mind of her own. However, the attributes of independence and knowing one's own mind, while positive ones to twentieth-century eyes, were not necessarily so to the biblical writers. Further, the biblical account is written from the point of view of the Israelites, not that of the Philistines (which is why Raḥab is honoured in the Bible,

45. D.N. Fewell, 'Judges', in C.A. Newsom and Sharon H. Ringe (eds.), *The Women's Bible Commentary* (London: SPCK; Louisville, KY: Westminster/John Knox, 1992), pp. 67-77 (pp. 73-74).

46. Klein, 'The Book of Judges', pp. 55-71 (62).

47. Klein, 'The Book of Judges', pp. 62-63.

48. Exum points out that 'she is not identified, as biblical women typically are, in relation to a man, usually, their father or husband. She appears to have her own house, but how she came by it is not revealed' (Exum, *Plotted, Shot, and Painted*, p. 181).

even though her sexual behaviour is questionable). In any case, this method is open to the objection that viewing Delilah in a positive light is only putting a different 'gloss' onto the story. A feminist reading is not necessarily helpful to women if it merely ignores their shortcomings and bad behaviour and only permits mention of behaviour and characteristics that are 'acceptable' from a feminist point of view.

Attempts to suggest that it is possible to read the story of Delilah in a more positive way can have only a limited success. However, it is possible to acknowledge Delilah's shortcomings, but argue that she is very much a victim of her time, and, given the limited possibilities open to a woman who apparently has no male protector on hand, as was customary, she does very well. Such a method attempts to 're-deem' the text from its original patriarchal setting and the patriarchal 'overlay' of years of interpretation. This involves looking at the history of interpretation of Judges 16. Nevertheless, the biblical text portrays various negative aspects of Delilah's character, and one cannot, with honesty, attribute all of the negative associations Delilah has had to patriarchal and misogynistic misrepresentations of the text, arising out of the world-views of the commentators. She does whine, wheedle and pester Samson. She does take money for betraying him to the Philistines. She does use the fact that he finds her sexually alluring to her own advantage.

Those who see Delilah negatively include, as one might expect, some very traditional authors. Many of those writing for a more devotional audience ignore Delilah, possibly because they find her too difficult to deal with in such a context. Others see in her a grim example. Here is H.T. Sell, in a 1925 book, *Studies of Famous Bible Women*, in a chapter entitled 'Delilah: A Temptress':[49]

> Delilah is a type of 'The Undesirable Woman'. She is a wrecker wherever she is and she is in every community. In her we search in vain for any conscience in regard to what she does or any pity for her victims... All her fascinations, and she has many, are exerted for the purpose of mutilating and destroying everything that is worth while in those upon whom she fixes her regard... It is the same old story through the ages. The methods of this woman, of this evil sort, remain unchanged... Why is this story in the Bible? It is not a pleasant one. It is sordid to the last degree.

49. H.T. Sell, *Studies of Famous Bible Women* (New York: Fleming H. Revell, 1925), pp. 38-40.

And so Sell continues. As far as this author is concerned, there is no question that there might be another way of looking at this narrative:[50]

> This story is left to make its own impression. There is no summing up. There is no moralizing. There is no preaching a sermon. The tale is sufficient in itself.

This view is echoed by Arthur Cundall, in his 1966 commentary:[51] 'The hypocrisy of Delilah, pretending to love but all the time plotting the death of her love, can be left without comment'.

J. Cheryl Exum, writing as a feminist, would argue that these two authors have caught exactly the agenda of the biblical writer in writing about Delilah and Samson's other women in Judges 14–16. This is, she suggests,[52] 'to control women and justify their subjugation'. Even what might be seen as one of Delilah's strengths—her powerfulness— is seen negatively by Exum since, she argues, women's power (which in Delilah's case is predominantly sexual power) is appropriated 'by an androcentric agenda to serve male interests'.[53] Exum speaks[54] of the biblical writer's perception that 'Women's sexuality must be controlled. In order to reduce its threat, women's behaviour must be regulated'. This thought echoes Nancy Tischler, who is very harsh about Delilah, describing her[55] as 'the cynical manipulator of sensuality' and making 'deliberate and calculated' choices. Tischler also makes the comment:[56]

> The multiple forms that the Delilah figure has taken suggest that it is one of the concepts of the female which haunts man and frightens him. She is no harmless plaything or mindless drudge; she is a real threat to his masculinity and his mission.

At first sight, Judges 16 might appear to be an absolute gift to those who wish to reject outright the relevance of the Bible for women, and for those approaching the story from a 'gender and culture' perspective. The narrator portrays Delilah as a woman who is prepared to lie, betray and use the fact that a man finds her sexually attractive to

50. Sell, *Studies*, p. 44.

51. A.E. Cundall, *Judges: An Introduction and Commentary* (TOTC; London: Tyndale Press, 1966), p. 177.

52. Exum, 'Samson's Women', p. 62.

53. Exum, 'Samson's Women', p. 89.

54. Exum, 'Samson's Women', p. 89.

55. N. Tischler, *Legacy of Eve: Women of the Bible* (Atlanta: John Knox Press, 1977), p. 75.

56. Tischler, *Legacy of Eve*, p. 77.

achieve her aims. Such a picture is not one that feminists would wish to have associated with women. Further, representations of Delilah in paintings, films and literature have intensified the portrayal of her as 'a temptress *par excellence*'.[57] Exum comments:[58]

> Delilah has become a trope for the *femme fatale*, the woman fatal to man —sexually irresistible, at once both fascinating and frightening, and ultimately deadly.

Exum examines representations of Delilah in paintings, Hollywood films, literature and musical works, such as Handel's *Samson*. She puts forward a convincing case for saying that there is masculine, and even anti-women bias in all the representations of Delilah in art and popular culture that she considers. Nevertheless, Exum's analysis falls short on many points. It is by no means certain that all those who see Delilah as a temptress and a seducer have seen either the paintings or the films that she mentions. They are more likely to have seen the advertisement for Weetabix, a breakfast cereal, that features Samson and Delilah. This piece of delightful nonsense, while it shows how advertisers assume knowledge of the story in the public's mind, nevertheless completely corrupts the story, because Samson escapes his fate, having eaten a sufficient amount of the appropriate breakfast cereal! (The fact that the story was considered sufficiently accessible to a television audience to make the advertisement commercially viable says a great deal about how far it has entered the culture and collective consciousness.) Exum also appears at times to be colluding with those she condemns since, while she gives an interpretation of the biblical story that shows how inaccurate many of these representations are, she ultimately moves away from the biblical text to cultural representations of it, thus focusing attention away from the text itself. She asks, 'Can women ever win, either in the biblical text or in its literary, musical, or visual afterlives? If not, why not?'[59] Her implied answer is that women never *can* win, and so there is no genuine search in her work. She already knows the answer.

It is also possible to take a more neutral view, suggesting that the narrative portrays Delilah *and* Samson as having both negative and positive qualities. My own view[60] is that this ambiguity about the

57. Exum, *Plotted, Shot, and Painted*, p. 176.
58. Exum, *Plotted, Shot, and Painted*, p. 176.
59. Exum, *Plotted, Shot, and Painted*, p. 8.
60. C. Smith, 'Samson and Delilah: A Parable of Power?', *JSOT* 76 (1997), pp. 45-57. My research for this *JSOT* article led me to write the current one, as I became fascinated by the different ways in which feminists had interpreted Delilah.

characters reflects other ambiguities within the biblical narrative that leave many questions open, and that the story of Samson and Delilah is, above all, a story about power—who has it, who uses it, and how it is used. As I have argued in a *JSOT* article,[61]

> while the narrative certainly does reflect the values and preoccupations of the patriarchal society from which it arose, it does not so much reinforce them as leave open the possibility that they may be questioned... Thus, while Exum may be correct when she says that 'Women's subordination to men is, after all, considered to be the natural state of things', it is not necessarily the case that this text (Judges 13–16) has as an underlying theme that 'the oppression of women is taken for granted' for all time.

I believe that Judges 16 is above all about the use and misuse of power by humans and deities and that both Samson and Delilah are seen as wielding power and also being manipulated by others who are more powerful than they are. Such a view is not incompatible with the feminist agenda. Questions about power have long been important ones for feminists. Much of our history has involved critiquing the structures of power within society and how they have operated to the detriment of women, and there is no reason why portrayals of the use and misuse of power within the Bible should be exempt from such analysis.

So where does that leave us? I think the problem is that feminist biblical scholars, for various reasons, have become far too dualistic in their thinking. And this may seem an odd thing to say in this context, as one of the accusations that has been levelled at the patriarchal establishment, particularly the academic establishment, is that its thinking is dualistic. And yet it somehow seems that we are being offered a choice: either be a feminist, and admit that the Bible is an androcentric, misogynist document that has as its primary purpose the facilitation of the oppression of women and the maintenance of patriarchy; or continue to attempt to reinterpret the Bible and give up all notions of calling yourself 'feminist'. And yet Heather McKay has rightly warned us: [62]

> Feminist strategies can only succeed if they are not assumed to contain all that is best in scholarship and if they prevent the critical pendulum from swinging too far towards a single-mindedly feminist stance.

---

61. Smith, 'Samson and Delilah', p. 48.

62. H. McKay, 'On the Future of Feminist Biblical Criticism', in Brenner and Fontaine (eds.), *A Feminist Companion to Reading the Bible*, pp. 61-83 (81).

Delilah: The Last Word?

So, is a feminist reading of the story of Delilah possible? Of course, but it may take many forms. A feminist biblical scholar is no different from any other biblical scholar. To be a *biblical* scholar she must start with the text. What does it tell us? It is a story that is universal, that has echoes of many other stories from many other cultures and ages. It tells of a woman with whom a strong man falls in love. He is so besotted with her that he will give her anything—even the secret of his strength, which must, of necessity, put him in her power. On the positive side, Delilah is a woman who achieves something that many others have failed to do: she brings about the downfall of the great Israelite hero. Feminists can point to this positive achievement. They may also deplore the methods that Delilah used. However, it would be appropriate to analyse *why* she operated in this way. What were the constraints on her that limited her ability to act in any other way? Were they directly related to her being a woman and the constraints on women of the time? Discussion of such matters is surely a feminist task. The fact that Delilah has been portrayed by filmmakers and others for so many centuries tells us something about the enduring quality of her story. It also tells us something about the importance of the Bible for our society and its influence on our lives. *How* she has been portrayed tells us something else about our own culture and the factors that have shaped us, and particularly about those who can be regarded as the shapers of our society. Nevertheless, examination of such depictions is a matter of feminist analysis rather than that of the feminist biblical interpreter. The task is important, but it is not the only one, and should not be seen as superseding all other methods of feminist biblical interpretation. The insights of those studying the history of cultural use of biblical images have something to offer to the biblical scholar, but they are not biblical scholarship. In the same way, the emphasizing of positive aspects of biblical stories concerning women, particularly in situations where the Bible is seen as authoritative, is legitimately the task of the feminist biblical scholar. As is the analysis of those texts which *cannot* be seen positively. What is needed here is a collaborative approach, and it is ironic that I should have to call for it, since one of the aims of feminists has ostensibly been to promote collaborative ways of working and show that they can be as effective as traditional, more competitive ways. Whether Delilah was delicious, delightful and delectable or deceitful, despicable and debauched—or maybe all of these—is for us all to decide for ourselves. I only ask that we listen to each other while deciding, and, even if we do not return completely to our feminist roots, at least remember them.

GOD OF LOVE/GOD OF VENGEANCE, OR SAMSON'S 'PRAYER FOR VENGEANCE'

Renate Jost

1. *Introduction*

The formulation of my title alone may be seen as offensive from a feminist point of view, since its language itself (especially with the German masculine article in the original) may strengthen the notion that God is male. In fact, I take the position that God transcends all gender roles; but, because the word 'Goddess' recalls feminine divinities in ancient cults and in other cultures, and still does not take us beyond the dichotomy of genders, I will for the time being retain the word 'God'.

In traditional Christian theology, the supposed 'God of vengeance' in the 'Old Testament' is regularly contrasted with the 'loving God' of the 'New Testament'.[1] But even a superficial glance at the texts shows that, quite apart from the fact that the God of the First Testament is also the God of the Second Testament, the witnesses of the Second Testament also testify to a 'God of vengeance' (cf. Rev. 6.10; 19.2) or refer uncritically[2] to depictions of a 'God of vengeance' in the First Testament (e.g. to Deut. 32.35-36 in Lk. 21.20-24 and Rom. 12.19-20).[3]

---

1.   For examples, cf. Erich Zenger, *Ein Gott der Rache? Feindpsalmen verstehen* (Freiburg im Breisgau: Herder, 1994); ET *A God of Vengeance?* (trans. Linda M. Maloney; Louisville, KY: Westminster/John Knox Press, 1996), pp. 13-22.

2.   On this see Zenger, *Ein Gott* , pp. 63-69.

3.   In some feminist circles it is the Goddess to whom limitless love and gentleness are ascribed: cf., for example, E. Sorge, *Religion und Frau: Weibliche Spiritualität in Christentum* (Stuttgart: W. Kohlhammer, 1985), p. 52. But texts that speak of the worship of goddesses show that they too can be linked with revenge and violence. In addition to the goddess of vengeance explicitly mentioned in Acts 26.4, let me refer here merely to the warlike features of the goddesses 'Anat—cf. M.-T. Wacker, 'Gefährliche Erinnerungen: Feministische Blicke auf die hebräische Bibel,' in M.-T. Wacker (ed.), *Theologie feministisch: Disziplinen, Schwerpunkte, Richtungen* (Düsseldorf: Patmos, 1988), pp. 14-58 (42-52); Astarte and Innana/Ishtar—cf., for example, Kaizer (Otto Kaiser, *et al.* [eds.], *Texte aus der Umwelt des Alten Testamentes.*

In turn, it is also true that the God of the First Testament is a God of love. This is a fact too little noted, despite the sufficiency of the evidence (cf., for example, Deut. 4.37; 23.6; Isa. 43.3; Jer. 31.3; Mal. 1.2; Ps. 146.8; Eccl. 3.12). This is true especially as regards the love of God for strangers (Deut. 10.18-19). Nevertheless, the impression remains (provoking revulsion far beyond the scholarly audience and those connected with the churches) that this God is also a God of vengeance. The notion of God as vengeful is a problem that arises in similar form in the ideas of God found in other religions as well.

In the context of Jewish–Christian dialogue Erich Zenger and Jürgen Ebach, among others, have undertaken to combat the charge that the God of the First Testament is a God of vengeance. Since they have opened some avenues for understanding, in the next sections I would like to describe their arguments and then, taking up their suggestions, to present my own feminist–liberation–theological approach to the problem of the idea of a God of vengeance in terms of an interpretation of the story of the 'superman', Samson.

2. *Toward a Hermeneutics of the Statements about a God of Vengeance*

Jürgen Ebach gives the following pointers for an understanding of the statements about a God of vengeance:

1. He begins with the notion of נקם, which is often translated into English as 'retaliation' or 'punishment', but more commonly as 'revenge' or 'vengeance'. One problem in translating this word lies in the fact that the scope of the English word 'vengeance' and that of the Hebrew נקם are fundamentally different. While vengeance is 'the expression of an emotion and in practice is an action outside the law',[4] the institution of blood vengeance laid down in several legal texts of the Hebrew Bible from different time periods is an element within the law.[5] 'Vengeance', נקם in this sense is inseparably connected with justice.

II. *Orakel, Rituale, Bau- und Votivinschriften, Lieder und Gebete* [Gütersloh: Gerd Mohn, 1986–1991], pp. 694, 699) and also Balz-Cochois (H. Balz-Cochois, *Inanna: Wesensbild und Kult einer unmütterlichen Göttin* [Gütersloh: Gerd Mohn, 1992], from p. 162).

4.   Jürgen Ebach, 'Der Gott des Alten Tesaments—ein Gott der Rache? Versuch der Klärung einer gerade von Christen immer wieder gestellten Frage', *JK* 3 (1994), pp. 130-39 (132-33).

5.   Ebach, 'Der Gott des Alten Tesaments', p. 133.

2. To call on God as avenger, according to Ebach, means resigning one's own right to vengeance and leaving it to God. According to the texts of the Bible, then, the oppressed, the poor and the exploited have a right to be avenged by God.

3. Ebach emphasizes that God's acts of punishment cannot be understood apart from God's loving and forgiving. God's grace vastly exceeds the divine vengeance: while the latter extends to the third and fourth generation, the love of God extends to the thousandth generation.

Erich Zenger offers a similar argument in his hermeneutic of the psalms of enmity and vengeance:

4. He points out that, in the psalms of vengeance, the petitioners scream out their suffering because of the injustice and hubris of the violent. It is true that the portrayal of God as a judge who brings about justice does not absolve any earthly court from also doing justice; but, in the cries of those who pray, it is painfully evident that 'human judges and courts are insufficient to establish perfect justice'.[6]

5. He interprets the meaning of Hebrew נקם much as Ebach does. In the psalms as well, those who pray appeal to a God who is to restore and defend the order of law that has been demolished.[7]

6. He points to the genre of the texts: the psalms are poems whose artistry is expressed primarily in their function as lament and accusation.[8] In specialized theological language, the psalms are said to be 'realized theodicy', because they attribute feelings of hatred and aggression to God as well.[9]

7. Zenger begins with the idea of revelation. Against the comparison and contrast 'God of violence = Old Testament/Judaism' versus 'God of love = New Testament/Christianity' that has repeatedly surfaced in the past and even today, he points out that each testament cries out for both divine violence and an end to violence. Fundamental to this point is that the Bible is not an immediate verbal revelation, but 'the word of God in human words',[10] that is, dynamic revelation.

According to Zenger this means, for a hermeneutics of the biblical texts, that:

6.   Zenger, *God of Vengeance?*, p. 67.

7.   Zenger, *God of Vengeance?*, p. 70; cf. Erich Zenger, *Das Erste Testament: Die jüdische Bibel und die Christen* (Düsseldorf: Patmos, 3rd edn, 1993), p. 62. Cf. also Ebach, 'Gott der Rache?', p. 135.

8.   Cf. Zenger, *God of Vengeance?*, pp. 76–77.

9.   Zenger, *God of Vengeance?*, p. 79.

10.   Zenger, *God of Vengeance?*, pp. 80–81.

(1)   The texts must be understood, with the aid of historical crit-
        icism, within their religious-historical contexts.

(2)   Biblical texts must be heard canonically; that is, texts on the
        same theme are mutually interpretive.

(3)   Because texts that in their origins were liberating may have
        had a destructive reception, their history of reception must
        always be taken into account.

(4)   Only the Bible as a whole is revelation.[11]

3. *Samson's 'Prayer of Vengeance'*

The Samson saga offers a good example, though scarcely noticed in
this connection, of the location in which a 'prayer of vengeance' might
be spoken. The fact that, at a superficial glance, the focus of interest is
a man need not be an obstacle to a feminist–liberation–theological
interpretation but, rather, a challenge, if such interpretation does not
wish to restrict itself to the few biblical texts in which women play a
central role. Being a feminist exegete means taking women's experiences as a starting point. The concept of 'feminism' also implies a theoretical, social-, epistemological-, and scholarly-critical level at which
patriarchy can be analyzed as the ultimate source of oppressive systems. Since patriarchy should be understood not so much as 'male
domination' but rather as 'paternal domination', that is, the rule of
some men over other men and all women, this analysis also concerns
men, though in a way different from the way it concerns women.[12]
From this standpoint, it is reasonable to include an interpretation of
texts in which men appear to be the center of interest and to inquire
about their significance for feminist exegesis.

Samson's prayer of vengeance concludes the narrative in Judges 13–
16. Samson is a failure. He has lost the strength attributed in the framework of the narrative, as we now have it, to the hair of his head and
thus to his status as a *nāzîr*. More than that, he has become an object of
ridicule to his enemies. He has lost both his eyes. In this situation Samson prays:

> Lord God, remember me
> and strengthen me
> only this once,

---

11. Zenger, *God of Vengeance?*, pp. 83–86.

12. Cf. Hedwig Jahnow *et al.*, *Feministische Hermeneutik und Erstes Testament:
Analysen und Interpretationen* (Stuttgart: W. Kohlhammer, 1994), pp. 9, 11.

> O God,
> so that with this one act of revenge
> I may be avenged upon the Philistines
> for one of my two eyes (Judg. 16.28).

Samson's prayer is heard, although at a price: he is buried with his enemies.

It is clear from the treatment of the text of this prayer in the oldest translations that not only modern readers have had difficulties with Samson's desire for revenge. While the Masoretic text reads 'for one of my two eyes', the Septuagint and the Vulgate both read 'a [single] revenge for my two eyes'. Does the Masoretic version put more emphasis on the fact that the 'revenge' to be exacted is more limited than it could be, while the Septuagint and Vulgate stress the full exercise of vengeance? Or, on the contrary, did the version in the ancient translations weaken a Hebrew text that expressed Samson's hope of being able to exact revenge for his second eye at a later time? In any case, since both the Masoretic and Greek texts are Jewish in origin, this is an inner-Jewish conflict.

Christian, anti-Jewish interpretations appear when Samson is negatively evaluated or even stylized as an antitype of Christ. Thus, for example, Hans Wilhelm Hertzberg locates Samson within the ranks of the men of God despite his 'unspiritual *habitus*', but then he continues:

> As one prepared from his mother's womb, dedicated to God, and gifted with the Spirit, he is a precursor in a still broader sense. Behind him appears 'the mightiest of kings', as the *Heliand* calls the Christ. The man who in his death killed more than in his life stands in striking contrast to Jesus, who with his death gave life to a world.[13]

Gerhard von Rad also describes Samson as one who bitterly falls in the struggle between *eros* and *charisma* and, thus, appears as the negative hero of a 'non-humane' and 'elemental' era.[14]

A. Graeme Auld goes the farthest. He asserts at the outset that he is not taking any position, but then falls into a classic anti-Jewish schema by making a generalizing contrast between the bloody and personal vengeance of the heroes of the First Testament and Jesus' ethics of forgiveness:

13. Hans Wilhelm Hertzberg, *Die Bücher Josua, Richter, Ruth* (ATD, 9; Göttingen: Vandenhoeck & Ruprecht, 1953), p. 234.

14. Cf. Gerhard von Rad, *Gottes Wirken in Israel: Vorträge zum Alten Testament* (ed. Odil Hannes Steck; Neukirchen–Vluyn: Neukirchener Verlag, 1974), p. 52.

Such bloody personal 'satisfaction' separates the heroes of the Old Testament and our own natural instincts by a great chasm from the ethics
of Jesus, who called for his Father's forgiveness for those who had inflicted on him sufferings much less merited than Samson's.[15]

We owe acknowledgment to the Dutch scholar Mieke Bal for having interpreted the Samson saga from a consistent feminist perspective. With the aid of structural narratology, Bal offers a psychoanalytic
analysis of the saga. She thus sees in the destruction of the columns
and the death of Samson the working out of his birth trauma. In her
analysis, the columns represent a woman's breasts.[16] The woman is
killed along with the rest of her tribe, and is thus made superfluous.[17]
That Samson is retrieved by his male relatives she interprets thus:
'Now he is allowed into the country of the circumcised, the pure, the
lust-free. Now the pact with God, the male principle, has finally been
realized'.[18] Problematically, in the interest of taking the part of
women—Delilah in this case—the author (Bal) has identified Samson,
death, God, and the male principle. There is a hidden risk here of
giving scope to anti-Jewish clichés.

The fact that other interpretations of the Samson saga and his supposed 'revenge' are possible is evident from the existence of readings
of Samson as a tragic spiritual hero, such as we find already in the
work of Josephus and in the letter to the Hebrews (11.32-33).

A meticulous theological interpretation by Cheryl Exum opens a
promising possibility for overcoming the cliché about Samson as a
man in covenant with God who exercises personal vengeance. Against
the interpretation of Samson as a failed hero, she objects that Samson
is not explicitly judged for his behavior. On the contrary: God appears
to have a finger in Samson's unbridled actions. She understands the
Hebrew נקם not as 'revenge' but, rather, as 'vindication'. Following
George E. Mendenhall, Exum explains:

> ...*nqm* is not vengeance which asserts the self as arbiter, but rather vin-
> dication, the legitimate exercise of force where the normal legal institu-
> tions of society are obstructed. Thus, Samson acts as the legitimate agent

15. A. Graeme Auld, *Joshua, Judges, Ruth* (Philadelphia: Westminster Press,
1984), pp. 221–22.

16. In a later interpretation Bal also interprets the same scene as a symbolic
rape (Mieke Bal, *Death and Dissymetry: The Politics of Coherence in the Book of Judges*
[Chicago: University of Chicago Press, 1988], p. 227).

17. Cf. Mieke Bal, *Lethal Love: Feminist Literary Readings of Biblical Love Stories*
(Bloomington: Indiana University Press, 1987), p. 62.

18. Bal, *Lethal Love*, p. 63.

of Yhwh's punishment—in this intance, for the ignominy YHWH's servant has suffered at the hands of the Philistines.[19]

Much like Ebach and Zenger, Exum was able as early as 1983 to counter the cliché of an 'Old Testament God of vengeance' by locating the meaning of נקם in a legal context.

Manfred Görg, who regards Samson's words rather as an invocation that calls for a 'remembering' (זכר, Judg. 16.28), for a rapid intervention by God, sees behind them the idea of the 'God who strikes', a notion also at home in Israel. This God destroys evil and its representatives. YHWH is thus said to be the addressee of a request for a liberating blow, such as is repeatedly uttered in human crisis situations. Samson's plea is not a model 'prayer' but, rather, reflective of the utterance of someone in that kind of situation who reacts in an all-too-human way.[20] I assume that an invocation can also be a prayer, and that I do not want to speak of Samson's 'lust for revenge'.[21] However and quite apart from this, I agree with Görg in the sense that in Samson's prayer YHWH intervenes as a God who takes the side of the dispossessed. Samson's prayer is heard because, robbed of his original strength and the light of his eyes, he capitulates—in the end—the one-time hero is a humiliated man. Now only YHWH can intervene on his behalf. Thus, Samson's situation is comparable to that of those who pray the psalms. Only the narrative context, the saga of the strength and ultimately the failure of the tragi-comic superman Samson, can be the measure of the depth of his prayer.

The historical context in which the narrative probably originated and was transmitted presents another point of departure for understanding it. The narrative reflects pre-national conditions while its final version was completed in the postexilic period: both times when Israel, or Judah, was itself threatened or oppressed by other nations. Told in such a context, a story like the Samson saga had a liberating character from the viewpoint of the humiliated; it said to them: 'God is on your side'. This reading is problematic when such a text is read in the context of the rich Western European and North American churches belonging to the dominant culture. Saying 'God is on your side' in this context would turn on their heads the statements about a God who is on the side of the weak. In the primary communities of Latin America, where marginalized women and men gather to draw strength

---

19. Cheryl J. Exum, 'The Theological Dimension of the Samson Saga', *VT* 23.1 (1983), pp. 30-45 (42).

20. Cf. Manfred Görg, *Richter* (NEB; Würzburg: Echter Verlag, 1993), pp. 86-87.

21. Görg, *Richter*, p. 86.

from the biblical stories for their struggle to survive, such a story looks different—as it does in the long history of Jewish suffering. In Jewish congregations, the Samson narrative can still be heard as an empowering story for a persecuted minority. But, even in a Jewish context, a changed political situation can lead to a problematic understanding. Thus an Israeli Jew has described as the 'Samson syndrome' the wish of some Israelis to destroy the whole Arab world along with themselves rather than permitting any approach to the Palestinian Arabs as their neighbors.[22] John Hamlin comments that it is the same attitude that threatens our whole world when it contemplates an atomic war that would mean the destruction of all parties in the struggle.[23]

Does, then, a reading of נקם, 'vindication' in a legal sense lead us not to the dilemma of a vengeful God, but instead to the dilemma of a God who demands violence to the point of complete self-destruction? No. For this very prayer of Samson and its being heard at the end of the narrative make clear, as do other texts in the First Testament, that the exercise of vengeance, the violent restoration of violated rights, is a matter for God and not for human beings.

From a feminist perspective, the Samson narrative itself can be read as an unapologetic critique of the attitude described as the 'Samson syndrome' because the narrative portrays Samson not as a hero worthy of imitation but rather as a tragico-comic figure. Samson only fulfills his liberating task when, through his own fault, he has lost the strength that made him a biblical superman; and is wholly dependent on having his prayer heard by God. Moreover, the completion of his mission is possible only at the price of his own death, the utter disempowerment of the once-powerful.

It is tempting to reverse the narrative perspective and tell the story from Delilah's point of view. Delilah could then be understood as a Philistine hero, much like Judith. But because a feminist–liberation–theological perspective takes into account not only gender but also relationships of domination this reversal is at least somewhat problematic, for Delilah is one of the Philistines, the powerful nation. Taking her part requires that, at the same time, we do not lose sight of her complicity in the oppression of a smaller nation.

22. Yehezkel Landau, *Jerusalem Post*, 11 August 1985. Cf. E. John Hamlin, *At Risk in the Promised Land: A Commentary on the Book of Judges* (Edinburgh: Handsel Press, 1990), p. 140.

23. Hamlin, *At Risk in the Promised Land*, p. 140.

Samson's mother could be seen as a female counter-figure to that of Samson. Although in contrast to her husband Manoah, to her son Samson and to Delilah she remains nameless, she is depicted as always trusting in God. It is she who encounters the life-giving power of God by which she receives new life, a son. Implicit in the narrative of the divine revelation she receives is God's love for the 'weak'. At the end of the story, when Samson is deprived of all 'manly power' and prays to God for 'vengeance', that is, for the restitution of his violated rights, Samson also experiences God's merciful love, paradoxically in his own death.

In Christian tradition the idea of this 'God of vengeance' is largely repressed, and replaced by the idea of a God who is entirely loving. On the political and social level, this can mean that we come to terms all too quickly with the injustices in our society and, in the face of the obvious deficiencies, sink into what Dorothee Sölle calls the 'profound depression of the middle class'.

By contrast, the faith that our God is also a 'God of vengeance', in the sense of restoring a broken order of justice, has a liberating effect. It makes it possible for us to accept our rage over personal and social injustice as 'the power of anger in the work of love',[24] in the words of Beverly Wildung Harrison. This faith can be a source of energy for actively doing the works of love 'to stop the crucifixions, resisting the evil as best we can, or mitigating the suffering of those who are the victims of our humanly disordered relations'.[25] For this reason, the faith in the God of love as also a God of vengeance is indispensable even for a Christian feminist understanding of love.

24. Cf. the essay with this title in Beverly Wildung Harrison, 'The Power of Anger in the Work of Love: Christian Ethics for Women and Other Strangers', in *idem, Making the Connections: Essays in Feminist Social Ethics* (ed. Carol S. Robb; Boston: Beacon Press, 1985), pp. 3–21.

25. Harrison, 'The Power of Anger', p. 20.

LETHAL DIFFERENCES:
SEXUAL VIOLENCE AS VIOLENCE AGAINST OTHERS IN JUDGES 19

Ilse Müllner

Some day there will be a Somewhere in which the Other will not be *condemned to death.*

Hélène Cixous[1]

1. *Disturbances*

In the course of her discussion of racism in the white women's movement, Christine Schaumberger observes that many authors begin their texts by manifesting anxiety about dealing with this subject.

> I too feel anxious when I try to either write about the relationship between racism and sexism, or discuss racism in white feminist theology. I have to force myself to do this, because I'm aware that in this situation, 'everything I do could be wrong', and that my reasoning could be full of holes, unclear, even abusive.[2]

When I discuss sexual violence, it is especially difficult for me to speak about structures of oppression besides sexism. In feminist discussions of sexual violence, it would appear that offender and victim can be more easily differentiated than in any other field of feminist critique; guilt, it would seem, has a logic all its own. Any investigation into this 'logic' runs the risk of reproducing the all too familiar patriarchal pattern of violence against women: blaming the victim. Was her skirt perhaps too short? Was the look in her eyes too coy or inviting? Even if the term 'victim' were found to be helpful in breaking out of this pattern, its use would immediately be criticized. On

---

1. Quoted in C. Olivier, *Jokastes Kinder: Die Psyche der Frau im Schatten der Mutter* (Munich, 8th edn, 1993), p. 10.
2. C. Schaumberger, '"*Das Recht, anders zu sein*, ohne dafür bestraft zu werden": Rassismus als Problem weißer feministischer Theologie', in C. Schaumberger (ed.), *Weil wir nicht vergessen wollen...zu einer Feministischen Theologie im deutschen Kontext* (AnFragen, 1; Münster, 1987), pp. 101-122 (102).

one hand, the term 'victim' both stigmatizes women who have experienced sexual violence, and alleges that they will repeat a certain behavioral pattern for the rest of their lives.[3] On the other hand—the label 'victim' leaves no room for any capacity to act and, hence, makes resistance impossible. Therefore, in order to avoid these two pitfalls, the term 'survivor' has been introduced into the discourse. Christina Thürmer-Rohr makes a clear distinction between the critical situation wherein a woman is made a sexual victim on the one hand—that is a situation in which her struggle to survive is often cynically viewed as complicity; and, on the other hand, women's complicity in creating and maintaining structures that make sexual violence a possible and plausible phenomenon.[4]

Women's movements worldwide have made the analysis of sexual violence and the struggle for women's right to control the destinies of their own bodies a number one priority. The 'paradigm of rape' has become the basis for the analysis of violent behaviors in society as a whole.[5] This paradigm, however, is dangerous insofar as, on the one hand, it reduces violence to sexual violence; and, on the other hand, it obscures the fact that the discussion on sexual violence may, in some aspects, serve the patriarchal system. In cases where the discussion of sexual violence reinforces domination, the question becomes one of other Others and one of differences other than sexual differences.

The view that sexual acts may be acts of violence did not originate with the women's movement. Patricharchal discourse too has seen sexual acts as acts of rape, which means that it is not women's subjective perceptions that have established the criteria for such a classification.[6] In both narrative accounts of sexual violence as well as in the realm of societal mythologizing, it is quite clear that portraying the *other* man as rapist serves the interests of domination. A feminist analysis needs to look critically at the relationship between the myth of the Black

3.   T. Schmidt, '*Auf das Opfer darf keiner sich berufen*': *Opferdiskurse in der öffentlichen Diskussion zu sexueller Gewalt gegen Mädchen* (Bielefeld, 1996), pp. 87-145.

4.   Cf. C. Thürmer-Rohr, 'Frauen in Gewaltverhältnissen zur Generalisierung des Opferbegriffs', in Studienschwerpunkt 'Frauenforschung' am Institut für Sozialpädagogik der TU Berlin (ed.), *Mittäterschaft und Entdeckungslust* (Berlin: Orlanda Väuenbuchverlag, 2nd edn, 1990).

5.   Cf. Thürmer-Rohr, 'Frauen in Gewaltverhältnissen', p. 32.

6.   On the difference between subjective and objective criminal acts in German law, cf. A. Strathausen, *Ver-gewalt-igung: Zu Soziologie und Recht sexueller Machtverhältnisse* (Münster: DVV, 1989), pp. 109-152.

rapist and that of the highly sexually potent Black male,[7] as well as to that of the Jewish rapist who is paradoxically labelled lascivious and unmasculine, which is one of the stereotypes of anti-Semitic propaganda.[8] Additionally, that sexual violence in families most often occurs in the so-called underclasses is one of the most common prejudices in Western societies, one which equates sexism with classism, and which serves to conceal domination. Thus, feminist discourse on sexual violence is caught between the Scylla of reproducing the 'blaming the victim' schema and the Charybdis of allowing its own arguments to serve the interests of domination.

The debate over racism and anti-Judaism in the white Christian womens' movement in the West has made it painfully clear that the necessity to concentrate on sexual difference as an analytical category should not be allowed to obscure the existence of other differences. Elisabeth Schüssler Fiorenza uses the term 'patriarchy' in the differentiated sense in an attempt to take this challenge seriously. In her most recent publications she has even gone so far as to adopt 'kyriarchial' as a subsitute for, or complement to, the perhaps somewhat vague term 'patriarchal'. She does this with a view to making it terminologically clearer that a feminist analysis should not only concern itself with the oppression of women by men, but also promote the development of appropriate resistance forms by coming to grips with the complex interrelationships between various structures of oppression.[9] Thus, when Susanne Heine criticizes feminist theologians for an 'almost monomaniacal fixation on feminist ideas'[10] that leads directly to anti-Semitism, she fails to take into consideration the pluralistic

---

7.   Cf. S.L. Gilman, *Rasse, Sexualität und Seuche: Stereotypen aus der Innenwelt der westlichen Kultur* (Reinbek bei Hamburg 1992), p. 30.

8.   C. von Braun, 'Zur Bedeutung der Sexualbilder im rassistischen Antisemitismus', in Inge Stephan *et al.* (eds.), *Jüdische Kultur und Weiblichkeit in der Moderne* (Literatur—Kultur—Geschlecht: Studien zur Literatur- und Kulturgeschichte. Große Reihe, 2; Cologne, 1994), pp. 23-49 (28, 47).

9.   E. Schüssler Fiorenza, *But She Said: Feminist Practices Of Biblical Interpretation* (Boston: Beacon Press, 1992), introduces the term 'kyriarchal'.

10.   S. Heine, 'Die feministische Diffamierung der Juden', in C. Kohn-Ley and Ilse Korotin (eds.), *Der feministische 'Sündenfall'? Antisemitische Vorurteile in der Frauenbewegung* (Vienna, 1994), pp. 15-59. When Heine reproaches feminist theologians for using the undifferentiated term 'patriarchy' (a term which in her sense refers only to the hierarchical relationship between the sexes), and fails to take into account approaches which in various ways try to work out differentiations, I suspect that she is misusing the anti-Judaism debate as a forum for her anti-feminist position.

nature of the approaches that critics of patriarchy have developed in the field of feminist theology over a period of many years.

Despite the complexity of the debate over sexual violence, I will attempt to discuss the acts of differentiation that lead Others to become outsiders within a society. I will also try to take a closer look at the tendency to equate various forms of oppression that have their origins in dissimilar social circumstances. In the analysis that follows I will be drawing on my research on non-anti-Judaic interpretations of texts from the First Testament that deal with violence, using results arising from the theological debate on racism. In light of recent German and Austrian history, it would not be appropriate to suggest that anti-Semitism can be put on the same level as racism:

> Inasmuch as anti-Semitism cannot be reductively explained as social Darwinism arising either from racist ideology or a strain of (secularized) Christian anti-Semitism that subsumed nationalistic cultural anti-Semitism or from anti-capitalist economic anti-Semitism, it would appear to be a phenomenon that needs to be differentiated from racism.[11]

Despite the fact that anti-Judaism, anti-Semitism and racism need to be analyzed as separate entities, I believe it is possible to point to basic similarities and comparable patterns in all three which, moreover, manifest themselves as behavior towards concrete Others.

2. Anti-Judaism in Feminist Analyses of Violence

There is little doubt that feminists who study the dominant system of violence can easily fall into the trap of underestimating and banalizing other forms of domination; or, alternatively, of becoming apologists for the present situation, perceived as dangerous, by comparing it to other social forms which are therefore stigmatized as being much more violent. Thus, historically oriented analyses of sexual violence contain references both to first testament narrations and especially to those texts concerning the law. As Susannah Heschel[12] observed in a brochure published by the Green Party of Northrhine Westfalia in 1989, texts from the Jewish tradition are sometimes used as sole historical reference, thus functioning as scapegoats.

11. L. Siegele-Wenschkewitz, 'Rassismus, Antisemitismus, Sexismus', *Schlangenbrut* 43 (1993), pp. 15-18 (16).
12. Cf. S. Heschel, 'Konfigurationen des Patriarchats, des Judentums und des Nazismus im deutschen feministischen Denken', in Kohn-Ley and Korotin (eds.), *Der feministische 'Sündenfall'?*, pp. 160-84 (165).

Both the selection and the interpretation of the texts reflect the anti-Judaic pattern which misjudges the Judaic tradition as particularly patriarchal. Feminist analyses of violence have traditionally, and often, relied upon Susan Brownmiller's classic *Against our Will*, which was the first book to deal with sexual violence both in a broader context and on a theoretical and structural level. In Brownmiller's analysis of the First Testament, the issues of virginity and the offence to the dowry institution assume great significance. 'With a clearly marked price tag attached to her hymen'[13] could be taken as a linguistically insensitive *faux pas*. In reality, the statement '...for a piece of damaged goods could hardly command an advantageous match and might have to be sold as a concubine'[14] is not to be found in any text. Brownmiller nonetheless sees the Jewish tradition as evolving in a positive direction, inasmuch as women who were raped gained increasing control over the social and economic consequences of this act.

Astrid Strathausen states in a study based on the history of legal rights: 'That a wife may be subjugated by her husband is made particularly clear in Jewish law'.[15] To say that 'the abduction of women was quite usual'[16] in connection with the—even to the community of narrators—repulsive and horrifying narration of Judges 19–21 is tantamount to taking seriously neither the difference between narration and history, nor the condemnation of those acts in the First Testament itself.[17]

More revealing than the statements made by feminist historians on this subject are, however, the observations they have not made. That Halachic texts—which, from a modern feminist point of view, are almost breathtakingly pro-woman—are never cited, can be explained by the fact that the Jewish sources are relatively inaccessible to researchers who do not read Hebrew or Aramaic. Moreover, a basic lack of understanding about interpretive pluralism in Jewish traditions has given rise to interpretations that lift quotes out of context in order to prove that the whole culture is misogynist. Non-Jewish feminist literature fails to take into account that the Talmud discusses the psycho-

13. S. Brownmiller, *Against Our Will: Men, Women and Rape* (New York: Simon & Schuster, 1975), p. 20.

14. Brownmiller, *Against Our Will*, p. 20.

15. Strathausen, *Ver-gewalt-igung*, p. 19.

16. Strathausen, *Ver-gewalt-igung*, p. 19.

17. Cf. K. von Kellenbach, *Anti-Judaism in Feminist Religious Writings* (American Academy of Religion Cultural Criticism Series, 1; Atlanta, GA: Scholars Press, 1994), pp. 95-96.

logical effects of rape on women;[18] that it discusses sexual violence not only in terms of the extent to which the woman resisted the act physically, but also in terms of whether or not she consented to it; and that the Talmud condemns marital rape:

> Indeed, far from treating a wife as a piece of property or mere object for the satisfaction of the husband's sexual desire, talmudic law may be the first legal or moral system that recognizes that when a husband forces his wife the act is rape, pure and simple, and as condemnable as any other rape![19]

Nonetheless, in the remainder of this article, I will be discussing the narrative, and not the legal tradition. The narrative I have chosen (Judg. 19–21) describes what is commonly seen as the most horrifying act committed against any woman in the entire First Testament: the rape of one woman by a horde of men, which leads to her death. Judges 19–21 tells also of war and 'abduction' (in reality mass rape), as well as untamed wilderness, boundaries and the crossing of boundaries. It is also concerned with group consciousness, and with alienation.

Efforts to avoid interpreting this narrative in an anti-Judaic way arise from two different attitudes towards the relationship with the Other. When discussing sexual violence, it is essential to perceive Others other than women in terms of differences other than sexual differences, and to look carefully at the interconnections within the dominant ways of dealing with differences. First, the text as Other should be taken seriously. In addition to that, the question of the relationships between various differences within the narrative world of Judges 19 has to be considered.

3. *The Text as Other*

As the cultural critic Tzvetan Todorov states, the European capacity to understand the Other, paradoxically, contains within it the danger of Eurocentrism. In seeking to gain a full understanding of the Other, the European risks giving in to the temptation of imagining the Other as a mirror of his/her Self and of his/her own suppressed Selves. The philosopher of religion Charles Long has coined the term 'opaque-

18. Cf. R. Biale, *Women and Jewish Law: An Exploration of Women's Issues in Halakhic Sources* (New York: Schocken Books, 1984), p. 245.

19. D. Boyarin, *Carnal Israel: Reading Sex in Talmudic Culture* (The New Historicism: Studies in Cultural Poetics, 25; Berkeley: University of California Press, 1993), p. 114. Cf. Biale, *Women and Jewish Law*, from p. 252.

ness' as a kind of antithesis to the term 'enlightenment'. 'Opaqueness' is used by Long descriptively regarding the self realization of the Blacks, who are constructed as Others. Subsequently the term is used normatively as relating to the perception of Others by the dominants, hence it describes the acceptance of the Other's opacity.

> It is primarily a question of acknowledging the Other as a person whom we perhaps cannot know either completely or even partially.[20]

This idea of otherness is carried over into the biblical text:

> All attempts to mitigate this Otherness, for example by 'modernizing' the translation, amounts to abuse of those texts by another culture, an abuse that is structurally similar to Western racism.[21]

The biblical text should not be allowed to become a vehicle for peering into the experience of women from other cultures and historical periods, not only because these texts were probably written by men (some women think like patriarchs too), but also because it is not possible to extract the experiences of women either from evidence of texts originating in societies with narrators of both sexes, or through reconstruction of 'F voices'.[22] Attempting to gain insight into the immediate experience of women is like peeling an onion in hopes of finding a pit. The difficulty of denying the need for this pit, which could provide the real and whole truth concerning women's experience, a need which lies beyond all methodological discretion, demonstrates that the analysis of Western thinking mentioned above is correct.

The experience of sexual violence has social origins also; interpreting and working through this experience, likewise, is governed by social construction. Certainly, indignation over the marital laws in the First Testament is understandable in light of today's experience, given the fact that marriage was expected to be the consequence of voluntary or forced sexual intercourse with any woman who was not engaged to be married (Exod. 22.15-16; Deut. 22.28-29). However, it is not possible to determine the effect of such laws (if they ever really have been in use) in women's lives; a first emotional reaction will have to be suspected as projection.

20. T. Witvliet, 'Rassismus und Eurozentrismus: Historische Einblicke', in Silvia Wagner *et al.* (eds.), *(Anti-)Rassistische Irritationen: Biblische Texte und interkulturelle Zusammenarbeit* (Berlin: Alektor, 1994), pp. 189-200 (198-99).k

21. T. Veerkamp, 'Die Bibel: ein "fremdes Buch"; in Wagner *et al.* (eds.), *(Anti-)Rassistische Irritationen*, pp. 21-24 (21).

22. On this subject, cf. A. Brenner and F. van Dijk-Hemmes, *On Gendering Texts: Female and Male Voices in the Hebrew Bible* (Biblical Interpretation Series, 1; Leiden: E.J. Brill, 1993).

In a horrific narrative such as Judges 19, acknowledgment of the text's opacity naturally gives rise to disagreement over explanatory interpretations. At the level of fable, the narrative is so fragmented that scholars have been trying for years to render this fragmentation coherent, at least at the textual level. But in so doing, they have not taken seriously the scandalousness of the narrated events actually present in the uneven Masoretic text.

The Septuagint has already tried to clarify one passage in the narrative that is ambivalent in its depiction of horror. Whereas the Hebrew text fails to make clear whether the wife is dead or alive when the Levite finds her, puts her on the donkey and then cuts her into twelve pieces with a knife, the Greek version clearly states that the woman is dead (v. 28). In the Masoretic text, the Levite is depicted as an accomplice to the murder of his wife; but the Septuagint resolves this tension, adopting the Levite's point of view as expressed in Judg. 20.5.

Throughout the history of Christian exegesis, scholars in the tradition of higher criticism have searched for a coherent original, and—without acknowledging as much methodologically—have tried to gloss over the horror of difference expressed by the text.

A first difficulty presented by the text is the difference made between violent heterosexual passion and homosexual passion. The men demand that the male guest be handed over so that they can 'know' (ידע) him; after this, his wife is raped. One of the interpretations, for instance, solves the problem by understanding already the demand of the men as a request for the woman only;[23] another releases the tension by interpreting the verbalized intention as not a sexual one.[24] The idea that the structure of the plot denotes—to borrow a term from higher criticism—irreconcilable tension, admits the conclusion that the critics have particular attitudes towards homosexuality as well as rape. The view of homosexuality as an exclusive sexual orientation and a way of life first emerged in our culture in the nineteenth century. For these critics, sexual violence primarily is made up of sexuality and passion; and it is not within the power of men who sexually desire other men to suddenly begin acting like heterosexuals. However, what is lacking here is the realization that in this context sexuality is

23. Cf. already K. Budde, *Das Buch der Richter* (KHAT, 7; Freiburg/Br. 1897), p. 131.

24. Cf. H.-W. Jüngling, *Richter 19: Ein Plädoyer für das Königtum. Stilistische Analyse der Tendenzerzählung Ri 19, 1-30a; 21,25* (AB, 84; Rome: Pontifical Biblical Institute, 1981), pp. 204-19.

being viewed as a violent weapon, despite the fact that the concrete relationship between sexuality and violence has yet to be determined.

The host's offering of his virgin daughter as well as the Levite's wife has led certain critics to alter the text. Hans-Winfried Jüngling[25] treats the Hebrew פלגשו ('his wife') as a gloss, thereby rendering it unnecessary for him to account for and interpret the discrepancies between the three versions (the demand for the Levite, the offering of the two women, and the rape of one of the women). This view also makes it possible for him to see both the host and his guest as heroes. Even as venerable a practitioner of synchronistically oriented new literary criticism as Mieke Bal takes liberties with the text in order to render it coherent. Her basic thesis is that, in this text, a conflict between the older patrilocal and the more modern virilocal system of marriage is being acted out. This is a plausible interpretation which, nevertheless, is rendered problematic due to the fact that all differences in the text are reduced to this one conflict. In this interpretation, the host's offer is seen as indicating his acceptance of patrilocal marriage and his rejection of the Levite's virilocal marriage. Handing over the wife enables the host not only to protect the threatened guest, but also to purge himself of the guest's strange, modern and immoral way of life. At the same time, this act oppresses the Levite with the law of the father, as expressed in the patrilocal form of marriage.[26]

4. *Differences in the Narrated World*

It is as seductive as it is dangerous to interpret this text exclusively from the viewpoint of the difference between the sexes. In her womanist interpretation of Judges 19, Koala Jones-Warsaw[27] takes exception to this attitude, linking the opposition of women as powerless victims and men as powerful aggressors to Phyllis Trible's interpretation.[28] Jones-Warsaw states that a white middle-class interpretation does not 'acknowledge other types of victimization beyond that which white middle-class females experience (that is, from male domina-

25. Jüngling, *Richter 19*, p. 211.

26. Cf. M. Bal, *Death and Dissymetry: The Politics of Coherence in the Book of Judges* (Chicago: University of Chicago Press, 1988), p. 92.

27. K. Jones-Warsaw, 'Toward a Womanist Hermeneutic: A Reading of Judges 19–21', in A. Brenner (ed.), *A Feminist Companion to Judges* (The Feminist Companion to the Bible, 4; Sheffield: Sheffield Academic Press, 1993), pp. 172-86.

28. P. Trible, *Texts of Terror: Literary-Feminist Readings of Biblical Narratives* (Philadelphia: Fortress Press, 1984).

tion)'.[29] This interpretation takes into account the fact that men, as well as women, are victimized. She thus also makes it possible for the reader to identify not only with the wife, but also with the wife's father, the Benjaminites and the Levite.

In my view, treating strangeness as a central category is the key to an interpretation that would attempt to clarify the differences contained in the text. Two words that the First Testament uses for foreigner/stranger need to be differentiated: גר and נכרי. Both the Levite and his host in Gibeah are referred to as גר, a word that poses difficulties for the translator. Martin Buber translated the verb גור as *gasten*, and the noun as *Gastsasse*. In both the German translation and in the secondary literature, the word *fremd* ('foreign') is used alongside the word *Schutzbürger* (a citizen legally protected against violence). At first glance, the latter seems to indicate a positive social status and in any case has the same connotations as it does in the story of Judges 19—the vulnerability of the foreigner and the necessity to protect him. The fact that the laws in Deuteronomy are aimed not only at the גרים but also at widows and orphans, who were social groups especially in need of protection, tends to indicate that these groups were not treated this way as a matter of course. That those laws offered such protection indicates that such protection was not taken for granted, and that the members of these groups in all likelihood did not feel protected. The central problem in Judges 19 is not one of material need, which the laws were primarily concerned with, but of the stranger's general safety. In his wanderings, the Levite was accompanied by his servants and domestic animals; he also had a good supply of provisions, including food and wine for himself and his attendants, as well as provender for his domestic animals. He also carried a reserve supply that would enable him to offer food and drink to the host in Gibeah.

Gibeah is nonetheless not the first place where the Levite is a stranger: he is so named even in his own land as well as in the hill country of Ephraim, from which he is fleeing. As a tribe lacking their own inherited territory (only after the time of the narrative were the Levites granted their own cities), the Levites were one of the endangered groups within Israel. A Levite was not only called גר; Levites were also closely associated with the term גר in certain passages.[30] The term

---

29. Jones-Warsaw, 'Toward a Womanist Hermeneutic', p. 181.

30. E.g. this can be found in Deut. 14.29; 16.14; 26.12: Levites besides the three classic examples from Deuteronomy's socially disadvantaged, the stranger, the widow and the orphan.

גֵר, 'stranger', expresses a relationship which is concerned primarily with lack of land and, by extension, with the notion of displacement. To treat strangers not, simply, as you would a native of your own land, but also to love them as yourself, is one of the central tenets of Israel's Torah (Lev. 19.34). This commandment of love derives from the experience that the tribes of Israel had when they themselves were strangers in Egypt.

Inasmuch as in Judges 19 the term גֵר, 'stranger', is not associated with material need, it can only connote a state of relative powerlessness: powerlessness and displacement go hand in hand. The Levite's woman is in jeopardy not only because of her gender, but also because she is the wife of a stranger. The narrative expresses the danger she incurs in terms of her being displaced; she is classified primarily in terms of her having traveled a long distance.[31] It is the undefined Outside, the Nowhere, that puts her in a dangerous position.

Indeed, the hazards incurred by the stranger as גֵר are part of the consciousness of the narrative, but not of the consciousness of the narrated characters. The Levite reacts negatively to his servant's suggestion to stop over in Jebus, remarking that Jebus is a strange city (עִיר נָכְרִי) where the people are not Israelites. The Levite's use of the term נָכְרִי[32] emphasizes the hostility towards the unfamiliar that underlies this image of a town full of non-Israelites. In so doing, however, he misinterprets the narrative situation. The so-called prejudice refrain (*Tendenzrefrain*[33]) 'And there was no king in Israel...' signals a historical situation of chaos, primarily characterized by a lack of solidarity among the tribes of Israel. The Levite is mistaken in his estimation of who in Israel was to be considered as Other. This error shows that social coding is an underlying factor in determining who is deemed Other, and that this code is not intelligible to all concerned.

31. Cf. Gen. 34; 2 Sam. 13.1-22. Both Dinah and Tamar leave their protected room. Cf. Mieke Bal's (*Death and Dissymmetry*, pp. 169-96) impressive linkage of displacement in the Book of Judges with the Freudian term 'uncanny' (*das Unheimliche*).

32. This term is best translated 'foreigner' (*Ausländer*). The 'increasingly unfriendly behavior towards foreigners' arose from the overwhelming political and cultural influence of the Assyrians and later the Babylonians, which in turn led to the exiles in the eighth century in the Northern Kingdom and in the sixth century in Judah. See L. Schwienhorst-Schönberger, '"...denn ihr seid Fremde gewesen im Lande Ägypten": Zur sozialen und rechtlichen Stellung von Fremden und Ausländern im alten Israel', *BiLi* 2 (1990), pp. 108-17 (114-15).

33. Jüngling, *Richter 19*, p. 59.

For the person who, unbeknownst to him or herself, is labeled as Other, this error can be lethal.

The confusing situation the narrative relates makes it virtually impossible for the reader to identify with one of the characters; and the fact that the characters described in the narrative are not given names has a distancing effect. However, all the characters are given positive and negative attributes, and all are both victims and offenders. Thus in this narrative, the usual assumption that victims are not guilty does not apply.

It is difficult to feel anything but sympathy for the *Levite* as stranger: he himself nearly becomes the victim of a violent act, and he also becomes a co-victim through the act of violence directed at his wife (v. 25). But he also takes on the role of offender when he thrusts his wife outside the house. In v. 29, shortly before the Levite cuts his wife into pieces, חזק ('hold') is simply part of the narrative—whereas in 2 Sam. 13.11, 14 it is part of the description of a sexual violence act. This treatment must in any case be characterized as violent. The semantic parallelism with the binding of Isaac in Genesis 22[34] also sets up a contrast to the acts committed by the Levite. Whether the Levite actually does murder his wife remains unclear. This ambivalence is an integral part of the Levite's characterization, and makes it difficult for the reader to identify with him.

The *Levite's wife* has become the quintessential symbol of 'victim'. That a woman who was a victim of such a violent act bears no name is so painful to some readers that they have given her one:

> I feel it not only acceptable but necessary to take some critical distance from the alienating anonymity of the character—without, however, losing sight of the structure of subjectivity that it signifies.[35]

She is raped (almost?) to death by a horde of Gibeah men, after which her husband reduces her to the status of a mere sign, or symbol. Although she is depicted as a פלגש, a status that probably does not correspond to that of a wife proper,[36] she is so important to the Levite

---

34. On this subject cf. Trible, *Texts of Terror*. ויקח את־המאכלת ('and he took the knife') appears in this form only in Judg. 19.29 and in Gen. 22.10. Only in these passages is the noun המאכלת used with the definite article.

35. Bal, *Death and Dissymetry*, p. 43, concerning the giving of the name 'Bath' ('daughter') to the daughter of Jephthah. Bal calls the anonymous woman in Judges 19 'Beth' ('house'). J.C. Exum, *Fragmented Women: Feminist (Sub)versions of Biblical Narratives* (JSOTSup, 163; Sheffield: JSOT Press, 1993), from p. 176, calls this woman 'Bath-sheber', 'daughter of breaking'.

36. The legal status of the פלגש is unclear. The word appears only in this

that after she leaves he sets out after her in order to bring her back. Nonetheless, the narrative does not hesitate to draw attention to her unusual ability to act on her own. The Levite's wife leaves her husband and goes back to her father's house. The text, however, expresses a negative attitude towards the morality of this act. I disagree with Bernadette Brooten's translation of the verb זנה (v. 2) as *zürnen* ('be angry with someone').[37] Moreover, I do not think this passage should be used to support the view that, in ancient Israel, it was to a certain degree possible for a woman to initiate a divorce. The current view is that זנה had connotations of sexual misconduct. However, it should not be taken to mean a transgression that is separate from the wife's act of abandoning her husband. The verbal clause that follows v. 2a should be understood as a subordinate clause. Moreover, the conjunction ו should be translated as 'inasmuch'. The Levite's wife's behavior falls into the category of 'sexual misconduct' (i.e. socially inappropriate) because she has left him.[38] Inasmuch as the narrative casts the Levite's wife's acts in a negative light, she is not constructed as a blameless victim.

The *host*, introduced into the narrative as a stranger who also comes from the region known as Ephraim, enters into a relationship of solidarity with the Levite. His hospitality towards the Levite makes him a sympathetic character in the narrative. Such behavior was quite unusual in Gibeah during this period and, as a result, the host comes close to achieving a hero status in the course of the narrative. However, it is he who suggests that the two women be handed over, an act which renders him considerably less sympathetic.

Even the way in which the *Benjaminites* are portrayed forces the reader to feel empathy with the fate that befalls them. Their refusal to hand over the guilty Gibeah inhabitants leads to a war and to the near-eradication of their entire tribe. The danger that, without women, their tribe will die out gives rise to countless women being subjected to further acts of violence countenanced by all of Israel (Judg. 21). Regarding black women, Jones-Warsaw writes: 'Like the Benjaminites we

---

narrative and in the narrative about the rape of David's פלגשים by Absalom (2 Sam. 16). However, I have decided to use the expression 'Levite's wife' because I like neither the very negative connotations attached to the word 'concubine' nor the condescending expression '[an]other wife'.

37. B. Brooten, 'Konnten Frauen im alten Judentum die Scheidung betreiben? Überlegungen zu Mk 10, 11-12 und 1 Kor 7, 10-11', *EvT* 42 (1982), pp. 65-80 (68).

38. Cf. Exum, *Fragmented Women*, p. 179: 'A woman who asserts her sexual autonomy by leaving her husband...is guilty of sexual misconduct'.

must decide whether we should stand in solidarity with our brothers, and at what cost'.[39]

5. *The Others and the Self*

The story has no heroes; nor does it allow the reader to differentiate clearly between offenders and victims. The violence portrayed is delimited by borders and differences. Violence is sexualized, and is not confined merely to sexual violence by men as offenders or towards women as victims. At first, the Gibeah men demand the Levite as an object of sexualized violence. The lethal difference between sexual violence committed by men against other men, and that committed by men against women, is that in the narrative the Gibeah men's demand remains at the level of narrated discourse and does not carry over to the level of narrated events. Thus, a feminist analysis of sexual violence must accept the impossibility of explaining away the disturbance caused by the same weapons against the foreign man and the foreign woman. However, do the differences between acts of violence against men on the one hand and women on the other hand, in this story, consist only of the difference between attempting violence and actually committing it?

When in 20.4-6, in order to persuade the other tribes of Israel to take up arms against Gibeah, the Levite briefly describes what has happened, he is clearly not talking about the Gibeah men's plans in sexual terms, but rather in terms of an attempted murder: 'They tried to kill me, but they raped my wife and she died' (v. 5). This statement is usually interpreted to mean that the Levite is exaggerating so as to justify the fact that he has handed over the woman. However, nowhere in his representation of the events does the Levite mention that he himself has thrust his wife outside the door. Thus, his justification of his actions is related to the events narrated in ch. 19, but not to his own account of these events.

If the sexualization of the violence with which the Levite is threatened is seen as the extreme humiliation of this man as Other, which consists of his being feminized, the reason for the non-sexualized nature of the Levite's description becomes clear. For the Levite, not only the sexual act but also the threat of it (in other words, being victimized by the act of feminization) constitute extreme humiliation,

39. Jones-Warsaw, 'Toward a Womanist Hermeneutic', p. 184.

which is why he fails to mention them in his own account. In this context, it is incorrect to interpret as homosexual desire the demand made by the men of Gibeah that the other man be handed over for the purpose of violating him sexually. The threat made by the foreign men is made less serious by means of feminization. Thus, being strange is transformed into another form of being Other. And it is this other form of being Other, being feminine, that makes it possible for the Gibeah men to get control over the Otherness by means of sexual violence. The stranger is cast out into a twofold border area, that is, into a state of total displacement characterized by strangeness and femininity. The strict refusal to blur sexual borders—as expressed in the prohibitions against homosexuality in Lev. 18.22-23, and as expressed even more clearly by the prohibition against cross-dressing in Deut. 22.5—creates the ideological background against which the Levite is threatened with feminization.[40]

Sexual violence, as represented in this story, combines the two aspects of Otherness—being a member of the female sex and being a stranger—and thus multiplies, not only adds, these aspects of Otherness. Strangeness and femininity overlap in the sexualizing of violence in such a way that the Levite and his wife become interchangeable objects. The Levite's wife becomes a victim of sexual violence because she is both a foreign woman and the wife of a foreign man: these two aspects of being a victim must be viewed as part of one phenomenon. The men of Gibeah are primarily interested in doing violence to the Levite, but they achieve this goal by attacking his wife. Initially weakened by discursive feminization, the violent attack on his wife has a direct effect on him.

Just as the forced and actualized act of violence against the Levite leaves him a double Other, so does the text reinstate him as a self, inasmuch as it negates both forms of being the Other. The text meets the threat of feminization with the second act of violence committed against the woman, an act whose subject is the Levite himself. The cutting up of the wife[41] negates the dynamic process of threat that, as it arises from femininity, brings this process to a halt:

40. Cf. T. Frymer-Kensky, 'Law and Philosophy: The Case of Sex in the Bible', *Semeia* 45 (1989), pp. 90-102, from p. 96. G. Braulik, *Deuteronomium*. II. *Kap. 16; 18-34*; 12 (NEB, 28; Würzburg: Echter Verlag, 1992), from p. 161, rejects the interpretation of this rule as sanctioning an assumed natural order. He relates this passage to the exchanging of roles by men and women in Caananite religious practices.

41. The parallels with both Saul's butchering of the oxen, which also gives rise to a war (1 Sam. 11.7), and with ancient Near Eastern texts, indicate that a custom related to warriors assembling in preparation for battle is being referred to here.

> As a metonomy for that which has no fixed place, the sacrificed woman
> translates the disturbing, threatening, and dangerous back into the sys-
> tem, giving it a fixed position which does not take into account whether
> the normative order is being affirmed or attacked.[42]

Through this act of semiotization, the body of the woman is desexual-
ized, perfectly and repulsively. With this act of violence, the Levite
affirms his solidarity with the attackers at the level of sexual difference and, in so doing, reaffirms his masculinity. With the call to arms
against Gibeah, the Levite reinstates himself in the community of
Israel and puts the men of Gibeah in the position of the Other.

Inasmuch as violence is committed against the woman two different times—once by sexualizing her, the other by desexualizing her—
the text constitutes a way of dealing with the double threat of her
twofold Otherness, namely, the elimination of the Other woman.
Thus, the spiral of violence remains unbroken. It escalates to the point
where it fits into the system of behavior towards differences consti-
tuted by the text, and perpetuates countless further acts of violence.

This interpretation shows that not enough has been said about the
possibility of finding an alternative viewpoint that would bridge the
gap between two issues: the 'rules of hospitality', and 'sexuality'.[43] It
is precisely the mutual stigmatizing of various differences that
perpetuates and forms the basis of patriarchal power relationships. It
is still true today that the stigmatization of the other man though feminization, as well as the stigmatization of the woman through real or
metaphorically constructed relationships between femininity and wilderness, strangeness or nature, are paradigms of domination oper-
ating in countless realms of patriarchal society. For example, sexual
violence among men in prisons is one of the most taboo problems in
our criminal justice system. It is neither surprising nor accidental,
then, who in such situations is made the victim and who is the offender. The victim is stigmatized; and the sexually 'passive' men are
feminized, not only sexually but also by being forced to carry out
activities that are unworthy of men. They are thereby degraded to the
status of women. As a result, 'real' men refer to their victims as 'the
girl', or give them female names. Thus, the masculinity of sexually

---

The closeness of the parallel of Judg. 19.29 to these other texts is a subject of debate: cf. Jüngling, *Richter 19*, pp. 236-41.

42. E. Bronfen, *Nur über ihre Leiche: Tod, Weiblichkeit und Ästhetik* (Munich: dtr,
1994), p. 321.

43. Cf. Budde, *Das Buch der Richter*, p. 131.

'active' men is not called into question but, instead, is proven by denying the masculinity of other men. In racist ideological systems, the
feminization of other men is also used as a strategy to maintain domination: 'Stereotypes of femininity, Jewishness and Blackness are used
to code one's opponents in order to undermine their credibility'.[44] The
feminization of the Other as metaphor is a means for gaining control
over the unknown and, thereby, over what is threatening. In the
fifteenth century, the comparison of the newly 'discovered' continents
to a woman to be abducted[45] went hand in hand with real sexual
violence against other women.

The narrative of Judges 19–20 reveals the great similarity between
the desperate behavior towards differences and the search for identity
that consists of the attempt to construct the self by distinguishing it
from Others. It is a male self in search of itself that needs to take cog-
nizance of, and deny, Otherness as a threat.

44. Von Kellenbach, *Anti-Judaism in Feminist Religious Writings*, p. 21.
45. Cf. illustrations in S. Weigel, *Topographien der Geschlechter* (Kulturgeschichtliche Studien zur Literatur; Reinbek bei Hamburg: Rowohlt, 1990), pp. 143-48.

REREADING THE BODY POLITIC:
WOMEN AND VIOLENCE IN JUDGES 21[*]

Alice Bach

> Every woman adores a Fascist,
> The boot in the face, the brute
> Brute heart of a brute like you.
> Sylvia Plath, 'Daddy'

Rape is a weapon.[1] Rape is a weapon to reassert the power of a man over an enemy. Rape is used to create fear in women. Across time, legend and history have mythified not the strong woman who defends herself successfully against bodily assault, but the beautiful frail woman who dies while protecting her 'innocence'. Victory through physical triumph is a male prerogative incompatible with femininity. Rape is a subject that has been exposed by feminist criticism in one literature after another. We have come to understand that rape is not so much a sexual crime as it is a means of physical, mental, and spiritual domination. So powerful is the impulse for feminists to identify rape, even within literary texts, that feminist literary critics have inscribed what Adrienne Rich has called, 'more than a chapter in cultural history', rather 'an act of survival'[2] in the process of analyzing rape narratives.

Exum challenges the biblical authors with her suggestion of female figures being raped by the pen—if not the penis.[3] While this suggestion may seem to exist totally within the realm of metaphor, it

* First printed in *Biblical Interpretation* 2 (1998), pp. 1-19. Reprinted with permission.

1. I would like to thank Melissa Wilcox for superb research assistance and insightful conversation during the writing of this article.
2. Adrienne Rich, 'When We Dead Waken: Writing as Revision'; reprinted in Barbara Charlesworth and Albert Gepi (eds.), *Adrienne Rich's Poetry* (New York: W.W. Norton, 1975 [1972]).

3. J. Cheryl Exum, *Fragmented Women: Feminist (Sub)versions of Biblical Narratives* (JSOTSup, 163; Sheffield: JSOT Press, 1993), pp. 171-202.

is more than a tour de force. Because reading is such an intimate experience, its form of violation is almost as frightening as a physical experience. The importance of Exum's oppositional reading is that it asserted her right to read representations of violation critically, skeptically; to refuse to remain the victim of the narrative force of the biblical narrator. If women can march through city streets to 'take back the night', then feminist critics can also 'take back the texts', or at least recognize what is at stake in the process of representing rape and the act of reading violence.

One way to reclaim my power as a reader, to take back the text, is to follow a synchronic strategy of reading. Synchronic approaches give the reader a great deal of latitude in making connections between texts. Central to such a semiotic theory is that the connections in the text have been made in the unconscious mind, as in my own recent connections between the accounts of ethnic genocide in Rwanda and in Bosnia and the so-called 'carrying off' of the women of Shiloh in Judges 21. My decision to employ a synchronic reading, then, stems from my desire to examine two related subjects: first, I shall look at biblical texts in which women are sexually threatened or raped, and second, I shall compare the violation of one woman in Judges 19–20 with the narrative that follows it, in which an entire group of women are victimized. Just as Freud rendered iconic dreams readable through language, so a synchronic critic sees signifying force in the gaps, margins, echoes, digressions, and ambiguities of a text. The silence about the women of Shiloh, both in the biblical narrative and in the interpretations of this text, is as loud as the silence of the women themselves, given no voice or no subjectivity in the narrative. In these current days of sexual atrocities toward women of genocidal proportion, I have explored their biblical story expressly to end the silence of victimized women in Judges 21.

To analyze the structure of associations that produce a new reading of the collective rape of the women of Shiloh in Judges 21, I shall build upon other recent literary readings by women (Bal, Exum, Keefe, Niditch) of the unnamed woman raped in Judges 19. The tragedy and violence of women's sexual experience had not been explored in depth until the moments of outrage expressed in Trible's *Texts of Terror* and in subsequent writings of Bal, Exum, and others. Bal emphasizes that the agents of the *pilegesh*'s death are as unclear as is the moment of her death. The act keeps being displaced from one man to the next. The contamination by collective guilt is obviously problematic to all readers. Bal focuses her gaze upon the body of the woman, the body that is 'subsequently used as language by the very man who exposes her to the violence when he sends her flesh off as a message'.[4]

Another kind of message is sent by the sexual violence committed by the Israelites in order to get wives for the men of the tribe of Benjamin. Judges 21 depicts two kinds of rape: the sexual rape of the women of Shiloh and by extension, the economic rape of their fathers and brothers, who are by ancient standards the offended parties. There is collective violation in both acts. While an event of rape is not acknowledged openly in Judges 21, it is encoded within the ambiguity, the indirections of the text. The result is to naturalize the rape. By reading against the grain of the writers' intention to narrate the carrying off of women as wives for the men of Benjamin as necessary and natural, one sees how the biblical authors, men who possessed both benevolence and reason, could inscribe a rationale for oppression, violation, and exploitation within the very discourse of the biblical text.

In my reading of Judges 21, I inhabit the border life of the text. I shall make use of the friction between the narrative in chs. 19–20 and the one in ch. 21, not privileging one over the other. My initial move is to scrutinize the cultural ideology that supports rape as a stock narrative device for disorder in the biblical narrative. Literary critics from various fields are currently engaged in a polemic over the function and meaning of rape in its textual representation.[5] I share a belief with many cultural critics that readers, like texts (and, for that matter, characters within texts) are always sites where pluralities intersect. So that the friction between the biblical concept of rape, or more usually 'not-rape', and our own intense feelings of abhorrence at the violation of the female body provides a major site for my reading. Reading

4.   Mieke Bal, 'Speech Acts and Body Language in Judges', in Elaine Scott (ed.), *Literature and the Body: Essays on Populations and Persons* (Baltimore: The Johns Hopkins University Press, 1988).

5.   There is a growing scholarly literature on rape, reflecting the consciousness of real-life rape as well as literary and metaphoric rape. See esp. S. Brownmiller's classic, *Against our Will: Men, Women, and Rape* (New York: Simon & Schuster, 1975); Roland Barthes, 'Striptease', in *idem, Mythologies* (trans. Annette Lavers; New York: Hill & Wang), pp. 84-87. For literary rape, see discussion in Bal, 'Speech Acts'; M. Bal, *Death and Dysymmetry: The Politics of Coherence in the Book of Judges* (Chicago: University of Chicago Press, 1988); Exum, *Fragmented Women*; Teresa deLauretis, 'The Violence of Rhetoric: Considerations on Representation and Gender', in *idem, Technologies of Gender* (Bloomington: Indiana University Press, 1987); Muriel Dimen, 'Power, Sexuality, and Intimacy', in Alison Jagger and Susan Bordo (eds.), *Gender/Body/ Knowledge* (New Brunswick: Rutgers University Press, 1989); Trudier Harris, *Exorcising Blackness: Historical and Literary Lynching and Burning Rituals* (Bloomington: Indiana University Press, 1984).

Judges 19–21 as a single narrative unit allows me to follow the progression of violence from the representation of one violated female figure (*pilegesh*) to the representation of a violated tribe of females (daughters of Shiloh), thus raising the spectre of the tribes of Israel as guilty of a brutal male assault, an act of gynocide.[6] My final strategy is to reread Judges 21 through the lens of the rape camps recently uncovered in Bosnia. And to fill the female silence in the one text with the witness from the other.

Writing the Body Politic on Women's Bodies

Depicting, narrating, or representing rape certainly does not constitute an unambiguous gesture of endorsement. The consciousness of what constitutes rape is very different now from what it has been in earlier times. One advantage of a synchronic analysis is that the reader can move forward or backward through time. Foucault is correct that 'the lateral connections across different forms of knowledge and from one focus of politicization to another (makes it possible) to rearticulate categories which were previously kept separate'.[7] Thus, a synchronic reading cognizant of cultural theory needs to inhabit both the insular territory of the biblical world and other cultural arenas where the practice of sexual violence has been represented, such as the genocide in Bosnia. This essay hopes to map the comings and goings between these sites.

When a woman is raped in the Hebrew Bible, who has lost respect, who is the offended party? The biblical narrator does not raise a literary eyebrow at either the Levite in Judges 19 or Lot in Genesis 19 for using women's bodies as shields to defend themselves against sexual violence. Nor does the Bible characterize as rape 'carrying off' women to become the wives of the remaining men of an offending tribe in Judges 21. So the Foucauldian story of rape as evidence of ubiquitous domination is suppressed. The threat of homosexual rape is averted in Genesis 19, but sexual violence toward the *pilegesh* in Judges 19 is *doubly* suppressed; its homosexual element is disavowed by the Levite

---

6.   To the reader who thinks the term gynocide is an overreading, an exaggeration, of the act of 'carrying off' the young women of Shiloh, I can say only that we shall never know how the women characters in the text perceived their predicament. The silence of the women in the text will be filled by each reader.

7.   Michel Foucalt, *Power/Knowledge: Selected Interviews and Other Writings, 1972–1977* (ed. and trans. Colin Gordon; New York: Pantheon Books, 1980), p. 127.

in his retelling of the story and the corpse of the *pilegesh* is defiled by the Levite himself after her ravaged body has been returned to him.

A standard cultural myth is that rape is an unavoidable consequence of war. Looking solely at modern times, we remember that rape was a weapon of revenge as the Russian army marched to Berlin in World War II. Rape flourishes in warfare irrespective of nationality or geographic location. 'Rape got out of hand', writes Susan Brownmiller, 'when the Pakistani Army battled Bangladesh. Rape reared its head as a way to relieve boredom as American GI's searched and destroyed in the highlands of Vietnam'.[8] Of course in modern times rape is outlawed as a criminal act under the international rules of war. Rape is punishable by death or imprisonment under Article 120 of the American Uniform code of military justice. Yet rape persists as a common act of war.

Since the focus of this article is to be the interweaving of modern gynocidal activities of war with narratives of rape and one of gynocide, let us look at the mirror story of a gang of men in Genesis 19 and Judges 19.[9] When one reads each of these stories as a linear narrative, emphasizing its beginning, middle, and end, one concludes that such a narratologic strategy is far from innocent. Viewed schematically the beginning of the story focuses the reader upon the details it offers and suggests that other details or reality is insignificant (e.g. the reactions of Lot's daughters to the pounding on the door or to their father's magnanimous offer); the events of the beginning of the story lead to the middle and set up a causal inevitability (the threatened Levite thrusting the *pilegesh* outside the door); and finally the story's end appears as the unique result of all that has come before. Most important in this seemingly logical progression of a linear narrative is that it creates a sense of order, as though the conclusion (i.e. the rape and torture of the *pilegesh*) is the only possible outcome. Unless the reader listens for the woman's story muffled in the gaps and silences of the male narrative, the reader becomes a voyeur, complicit with the orderly retelling of the story. While listening to the silence is one effective narratological strategy for moving outside the power of the text,

8. Brownmiller, *Against our Will*, p. 32.

9. I have resisted supplying a name for the *pilegesh*, as Bal and Exum have done. Bal calls her Beth; Exum Bath-sheber. The anonymity of her namelessness creates a problem for the reader trying to identify her in a retelling of the narrative. This very difficulty underscores the gap or silence created by the biblical storyteller. By referring to her as *pilegesh* I hope to maintain the narratorial vagueness and lack of subjectivity that anonymity of a character presents in a story.

the reader can also examine narrative elements that aid the storyteller in the representation of rape.[10]

One narrative element provides a first clue: night, *laylāh*, the dark time of abandon. The two parallel stories of men threatening men occur at night: the men of Sodom call out to Lot, 'Where are the men who came to you *tonight*?' (Gen. 19.5) The Benjaminites also come knocking at night. They 'know' the woman all through the night, a continuous connection of nighttime horror, when men turn into ogres. As Bal so memorably characterizes this scene: 'she dies several times, or rather, she never stops dying'.[11] But the classification of even this rape, which seems so explicitly violation to a modern reader, is not clearly rape in the context of ancient law. Remember, the Levite *gave* the woman over to the mob. Compare another night scene earlier in the book of Judges: a Gazite mob lies in wait all through the night for Samson at the city gate, but they do not try to kill him עד־אור הבקר, 'until the coming of the dawn'. The difference between the two situations is twofold: the Gazites' plan to capture Samson fails, and secondly, they evidence no sexual designs upon Samson. The male victim is also the male hero. He survives, indeed, he triumphs.

Night is not always a sign in biblical texts for dangerous, loathsome acts. Night is figured as the time for important dreams, from the wrestling of the Jacob with the angel to the apocalyptic dreams of Zechariah: ראיתי הלילה והנה־איש רכב על־סוס אדם, 'In the night I saw a man riding on a red horse!' (1.8). The medium at Endor has her visions at night (1 Sam. 28). But the dreams of Zechariah and the woman at Endor are embedded with symbols of death. Usually it is the horrors of battle that occur in the light of day. Needless to say these are usually victories for Israel, not negatively signed acts. The taking of the young women of Shiloh in Judges 21 occurs in the daylight. Thus, one has the first indication of difference between the individual occurrences involving Lot and the Levite from the unified act of the Benjaminites taking wives from the virgins of Jabesh-Gilead and of Shiloh. Getting wives for Benjamin is a victory for Israel: not

10. Another subtle reference to rape comes from the mother of Sisera (Judg. 5.30) standing at the window, waiting for her son, triumphant in war. She waits for him to bring her 'spoil of dyed stuffs embroidered, two pieces of dyed work embroidered for my neck as spoil'. And without a shiver, she wonders about her son and the other victors: 'Are they not finding and dividing the spoil? A girl or two for every man; spoil of dyed stuffs for Sisera?' The irony of the text as traditionally interpreted comes from the fact that Sisera is dead, not that a woman is serenely imagining the rape of other women.

11. Bal, 'Speech Acts', p. 2.

against a foreign enemy, but a triumph that reunites the tribes, the men of Israel.

It is crucial to ask of a historical period whose literature is given over to the covenant between its members and God, how rape can function as a stock device and what is the relation this genre bears to gender? While several female characters are raped in biblical narrative—Dinah, David's daughter Tamar, the unnamed *pilegesh*—the rape least dwelled upon narratively by recent interpreters is the national rape of the daughters of Shiloh, initiated by the tribes of Israel. The text does not even name the action as rape. It is figured as a political necessity, not a sexual crime. Indeed the elders have created a problem for themselves through an ill-conceived vow: מה־נעשה להם לנותרים לנשים ואנחנו נשבענו ביהוה לבלתי תת־להם מבנותינו לנשים 'What shall we do for wives for those who are left, *since we have sworn by the Lord* that we will not give them any of our daughters as wives?' (Judg. 21.7). To understand the cleverness of this surface-seeming foolish vow, one must look at the double misreading of the Levite, who both covers up sexual violence (to himself) and uncovers it (to the *pilegesh*). It is up to the reader to recover the reading that denigrates women. Through a rereading of ancient narratives about male brutality towards women, I believe it is possible to envision rape as more than a symptom of war or even evidence of its violent excess.

Ovid's *Metamorphoses* offer an example of another ancient Mediterranean text built upon the representation of sexual violence. The Latin text retells the rape or attempted rape of many individual mythic women, among them Daphne, Europa, Syrinx, Arethusa, Thetis, Galatea, Pomona, Persephone, and Callisto. Unlike the narrator/storyteller of the biblical rape events, Ovid's narrator systematically focuses on the victim's pain, horror, humiliation, and grief. Ovid highlights the cruelty of sexual violation, showing the part of violence and degradation as clearly as the erotic element. Curran observes that rape is sometimes used by Ovid as a strategy to remind the reader that 'whatever else is going on in the foreground, rape is always present or potential in the background'.[12] I would counter Curran's support of Ovid's depiction of rape with the caution that the goddesses and mortal women who were victims of these rapes rarely suffered serious consequences beyond getting pregnant and bearing a child—serving to move the story line forward. Lest the reader be left with the

---

12. Leo Curran, 'Rape and Rape Victims in the Metamorphoses', *Arethusa* 2 (1978), pp. 213-41.

idea of great sensitivity to rape in ancient classical myths, it is important to note that Ovid also wrote in his version of the rape of the
Sabine women, 'Grant me such wage and I'll enlist today', adding a
flippant but not unheard of note to his other descriptions of rape in
ancient Rome.

In contrast to the use of rape as a metaphor for social dissolution or
for male warrior codes, in the Greek mythic texts rape is often used as
a device to portray the enormous sexual prowess of the gods. Even
when Semele is immolated after being penetrated by Zeus's lightning
bolt, the mortal woman's pain and fear are not part of the story. The
male-focused story continues as does the life of her unborn fetus,
Dionysus, who is brought to term in his father's thigh. The immola-
tion is blamed on the jealousy of Hera; the nurturing and birthing of
Dionysus is attributed to Zeus. Hera herself had an ingenious way of
annually recovering her virginity by bathing in a sacred river.

In medieval French romances rape is not presented as the malevo-
lent act pictured by Ovid, but rather is mystified and romanticized.
Rape is viewed as a permissible act of manhood, woman as warrior's
booty. Chrétien de Troyes, for example, systematically shifts away
from the literal representation of the female experience of violence
toward the moral, erotic, and symbolic meaning rape holds for male
characters. While Chrétien admittedly tends to rosy up rape in the
Chevalier de Lion, he embeds the legal codification of rape evidence:
the woman fought back, she tried as hard as she could to get away,
she resisted—such are the proofs required of a woman prosecuting a
man in medieval rape trials.[13]

Returning to the biblical stories of rape or attempted rape, let us see
if any of these proofs are evidenced. Annette Kolodny describes a
critical position that corresponds to mine in comparing rape narratives in the Hebrew Bible. 'The power relations inscribed in the form
of conventions within our literary inheritance...reify the encodings of
those same power relations in the culture at large'.[14] Women do not
fight back, they do not try to get away, indeed the women's struggles
and pain are not narrated. Women, even the violated ones, are as
silent, compliant, as uninvolved as the narrator understands them to

---

13. Kathryn Gravdal, *Ravishing Maidens: Writing Rape in Medieval French Literature and Law* (Philadelphia: University of Pennsylvania Press, 1991), p. 42.

14. Annette Kolodny, 'Dancing in the Minefields: Some Observations on the
Theory, Practice, and Politics of a Feminist Literary Criticism'; reprinted in
R. Warhol and D. Hernoth (eds.), *Feminisms: An Anthology of Literary Theory and
Criticism* (New Brunswick: Rutgers University Press, 1993), pp. 96-113 (97).

be. For in biblical law, rape is a crime against the father or husband of the woman. A woman has no right to initiate a trial. While Dinah's brothers exact retribution from Shechem and Absalom from Amnon, there is no articulated remorse on the part of biblical rapists. There is only one woman who screams 'rape', and retells her story quite volubly and graphically to her husband and to her servants. One remembers from Genesis 39, through the narrative of the wife of Potiphar accusing Joseph of raping her, that a woman in the Bible is supposed to be hysterical and outraged at rape. While the Egyptian woman behaves in the accepted manner, it is all a sham, her hysterics histrionics, as the audience knows full well that the woman is lying about rape. And we remember her as the narrator wants us to, a seductive woman asking for sex.

Writing Hatred upon the Body Politic

As I have noted, what I am referring to as rape in Judges 21 is not referred to as such in the Hebrew narrative. Instead of creating disorder in the biblical narrative as similar acts have in Latin or medieval narratives, these biblical instances of sexual violence are misread by interpreters as political exigencies. Finding enough virgins to wive the men of Benjamin is a political problem that men need to solve. Jabesh-Gilead has been defeated in battle, so carrying off their daughters requires no justification.[15] The arena of war (whether it be holy war or

---

15 . The classical interpretation understands the carrying off of the women of Shiloh as part of a 'holy war', sanctioned by YHWH and a reflection of the tribal confederation. The amphictyony theory has been discredited by most scholars. However, much of this scholarship has remained unchallenged in relation to the narratives in Judges 21, being part of a holy war, and thus inevitable and justifiable. See von Rad's foundational study of holy war in which he argues that an amphictyony-type confederation of the Israelite tribes is both political and cultic. (*Der heilige Krieg im alten Israel* [Zürich: Zwingli, 1951]). Smend's study modifies von Rad's theory, assuming that the amphictyony before Samuel was solely cultic and neither political nor military (*Yahweh War and Tribal Confederation* [Nashville: Abingdon Press, 1970]). For a review of the many views of holy war in the ancient Near East, see Moshe Weinfeld, 'Divine Intervention in War in Ancient Israel and in the Ancient Near East', in H. Tadmor and M. Weinfeld (eds.), *History, Historiography, and Interpretation* (Jerusalem: Magnes Press, 1983). S. Niditch ('The "Sodomite" Theme in Judges 19–20: Family, Community, and Social Integration', *CBQ* 44 [1982], pp. 365-78) questions the amphictyony theory but settles for half a cake, reading Judg. 19–21 as 'the acting out of this sort of justified holy war situation in a symbolically charged, rich narrative medium' (p. 375). A concise

civil war) provides men with the perfect psychologic backdrop to give vent to their contempt for women. Whether narrative rape or actual gynocidal violence, rape in war is a familiar act with a familiar excuse.

If this argument seems too harsh, look at the narrative, the male explanation for male action. The only narratorial concern at the outcome of the Shiloh incident is that the act of taking these girls must not be misunderstood by the males of the clan. So the elders instructed the Benjaminites, saying, לכו וארבתם בכרמים, 'Go and *lie in wait* in the vineyards', and watch; when the young women of Shiloh come out to dance in the dances, then ויצאתם מן־הכרמים וחטפתם לכם איש אשתו מבנות שילו והלכתם ארץ בנימן '*come out* of the vineyards and each of you *carry off* a wife for himself from the young women of Shiloh, and go to the land of Benjamin' (Judg. 21.21). The verbs ארב, 'ambush' and חטף, 'carry off' are violent physical actions that contrast sharply with the whirling of the women's celebratory dance. The verb ארב embodies both physical harm and action against an enemy; it is used to describe the Philistines lying in wait to ambush Samson until Delilah successfully binds him, ויסבו ויארבו־לו כל־הלילה בשער העיר (Judg. 16.2). The narrator relates that Joshua must ambush (ארב) ʿAi and its king as he did at Jericho, 'when Joshua and all Israel saw that the ambush had taken the city' (Josh. 8.21). Both these uses of ארב (ambush) differ from its use in Judges 21 in that ambushing a national enemy is the context in the Samson and Joshua texts. It is the women of Shiloh who are to be ambushed in Judges 21. This ambushing of women goes back to the model of the heroic rape, where the desire for women and violence to women go hand in hand.

The only other biblical use of the verb חטף is found in Psalm 10, יארב במסתר כאריה בסכה יארב לחטוף עני יחטף עני במשכו ברשתו ('they lurk in secret like a lion in its covert; they lurk that they may carry off the poor', v. 9). In Psalm 10 חטף is also used in combination with ארב. Both scenes evoke images of violence performed by a powerful party against a poor or helpless one. In the Psalm God is expected to intercede against the jackals terrorizing the poor. Presumably the women of Shiloh have no need of rescue; they have the Benjaminites as husbands.

It is a struggle to sympathize with the men of Israel even if their confederation is endangered. For the men of Israel in Judges 21 are never the ones who are in danger. Indeed, wiving the Benjaminites is

review of the scholarly chain of argument appears in Ben Ollenburger's introduction (1-34) to the English translation of von Rad's *Holy War in Ancient Israel* (Grand Rapids: Eerdmans, 1991).

a problem on account of another of those foolish male vows that results in women being sacrificed to protect male honor. As the Israelites conceive their plan, 'if their fathers or their brothers come to complain to us, we will say to them, "Be generous and allow us to have them; because we did not capture in battle a wife for each man. But neither did you incur guilt by giving your daughters to them"' (Judg. 21.22). The traditional understanding is that the Israelites had to be united as twelve tribes, to keep their covenant with God. Since they had vowed not to give Benjamin their daughters as wives, how could they then ensure that the tribe would survive? After annexing the virgins of Jabesh-Gilead there is still a shortfall. To tidy up the mess, the men devise a plan to wive the girls of Shiloh. Dancing perhaps the same ritual as the friends of the daughter of Jephthah, who had suffered mortally from a father's foolish vow, now the girls of Shiloh are to be sacrificed, not killed but taken as wives. Taken *as wives*—the escape clause that naturalizes the violent action and even lets their fathers off the hook, since they had not offered them as wives to the offensive, but still 'men of Israel', Benjaminites. Once again women have been the victims in a male shell game of sexual violence.

What might be interpreted by a modern reader as the nefarious plundering of the females ripening in the vineyards at Shiloh is obliquely connected by the biblical narrator to each man doing what was right in his own eyes. Perhaps the repetition of this phrase is meant as a promonarchic statement studded with sarcasm. Perhaps the phrase is a clear-eyed assessment of the importance of inter-tribal loyalties with a wink at sexual politics. At best the reader is nudged toward an interpretation unfriendly to the tribes' resolution of their problem. But can a feminist critic let the biblical narrator soothe the reader as easily as he plans to soothe the fathers and brothers of the maidens of Shiloh? The well-known call to arms of Helene Cixous reminds me of an obligation as readers:

> Language conceals an invincible adversary because it is the language of men and their grammar We must not leave them a single place that's any more theirs alone than we are.

From a feminist viewpoint the biblical understanding of rape and its punishment serve to show an asymmetrical relationship between women and men, coding sexual violence in ways that make it culturally acceptable. A second hint that the foolish vow resulting in the carrying off of the Shiloh women may not have been so foolish. The narrative raises the question of rape or seizing of women as an expected outgrowth of war. Triumph over women by rape is also a way to measure victory, 'part of a soldier's proof of masculinity and success, a tangible reward for services rendered'.[16] The neat resolution of the entire story of reading in Judges 19–21 also helps to bury deep within the literary unconscious the memory of homosexual attack.

One more category of rape augments my intertextual reading of Judges 21. In the minds of the male formulators of the story and their ideal audience, the horror of homosexual rape is far greater than that of a male violating a female. Substituting the violence done to himself with violence to the *pilegesh* explains the Levite's rage. Unharmed himself, he retains honor and standing within the community, enough to be able to incite the other tribes to violence against Benjamin. Unsanctioned male sexual appetite can ignite the proper rage of all Israel and does result in the vow to cut off the tribe of Benjamin, that is, to ensure that Benjamin loses its power among the tribes. But had the Levite himself been the victim of rape, the shame and humiliation would have been too great for him to have related his story publicly as he does in Judges 20. Further, it would have been unthinkable to have readmitted Benjamin as a tribe had its crime been a taboo that smashed sexual boundaries instead of merely stretching them.

The key semes that generate this reading are those of substitution, of offering the woman in place of the male in both Genesis 19 and in Judges 19, of offering the Levite's version of the story in Judges 20 in place of the one the reader has just witnessed in stunning detail in Judges 19. The version of the homosexual attack in Genesis reveals some important clues about the nature of the offer and of the substitution. Lot goes out the door and shuts the door after him, so he is on the same side of the door as the men. The door is clearly a sexual boundary Then he pleads with the men: 'I beg you, my brothers, do not act so wickedly' (Gen. 19.7). He offers his two virgin daughters in place of himself, but the bedeviled men press hard against him. Their nefarious act is stopped by the angels. Divine intercession restores Lot to the proper side of the door and rescues him at the last moment from narrative destruction. The divine narrator sends a strong symbolic message by blinding the men who would look and lust after what is forbidden to them (19.11). Nowhere in this Genesis text is a female substituted for a male. It takes divine intervention to halt homosexual intercourse. God responds furiously by destroying the Sodomites who

16. Brownmiller, *Against our Will*, p. 33.

would break through that door, that taboo, that binds men in community in the Hebrew Bible.[17]

What is the situation in Judges 19? The Levite and his host were enjoying themselves much as the Levite had recently enjoyed himself with the father of his *pilegesh*. The men of the city, a perverse lot, surrounded the house, and pounded on the door: ויאמרו אל־האיש בעל הבית הזקן לאמר הוצא את־האיש אשר־בא אל־ביתך ונדענו, 'They said to the old man, the master of the house, "Bring out the man who came into your house, so that we may have intercourse with him"' The Levite made no move. The Ephraimite went outside as had Lot, to try to deal with the men: ויצא אליהם האיש בעל הבית ויאמר אלהם אל־אחי אל־תרעו נא אחרי אשר־בא האיש הזה אל־ביתי אל־תעשו את־הנבלה הזאת, 'No, my brothers, do not act so wickedly', pleads the Ephraimite, 'since this man is my guest do not do this vile thing' (Judg. 19.22-23). The repetition is intentional; the one text recalls the other. Men threaten other men by pounding on the door. The door that leads to death is the boundary, the shield. In this account the Levite never risks death going outside the door, but rather, the Levite seizes his *pilegesh*, and 'pushes her outside' to the waiting mob on the other side. Can we consider the Benjaminites' act rape if the Levite handed her over to them?

In his version of the story that he tells in Judges 20, the Levite states that the men of the mob intended to kill him. So he gave them the *pilegesh*. But there is a piece missing: there is a lack of logic that is unquestioned by the other men, the narrator, or most interpreters. Why was the mob satisfied by the offer of the *pilegesh*? In Genesis 19, the mirror of the story, the mob rejected the offer of the daughters. It took divine intercession to protect Lot from homosexual rape. Divine intervention was not afforded the Levite.[18] Perhaps that explains the Levite's murderous rage. Could the rape of one woman initiate total tribal warfare in Israel?[19] Is the ensuing battle an uniterated *herem* as

---

17. I would like to call attention to Wilson's reading from a queer perspective. She emphasizes that the sin of Sodom is not that of homosexual threat, but rather that of ethnic and sexual violence (Nancy Wilson, *Our Tribe: Queer Folks, God, Jesus and the Bible* [San Francisco: HarperCollins, 1995], pp. 168-69). Her suggestion that the 'same-sex male-appearing angels' at the door in Gen. 19 are gay, and thus, are the potential victims of the story, is an intriguing example of gap-filling with one's ideological position.

18. One has the same narratological pattern in parallel stories in Gen. 22, where divine intervention halts child sacrifice of a male child and Judg. 11–12, where there is no divine intervention to rescue a female child.

19. Alice Keefe, 'Rapes of Women/Wars of Men', *Semeia* 61 (1993), pp. 79-97.

Niditch suggests?[20] Perhaps the Levite knew the confederation could
not cut off Benjamin as easily as he could cut up the *pilegesh*. Perhaps
the Judges' version of the story has been inverted to protect the men
of Israel from the specter of sodomy. Are there any further textual
clues about denying homosexual rape? Back to the *pilegesh*. In the
morning, she is unable to return to the 'safe' site even after the Levite
opens the door. The Levite shows no emotion at seeing her collapsed
form on the threshold. He also appears to think she is alive. Why else
would he command her to get up? Thus, the violated woman, perhaps by this time a corpse, *nᵉbēlāh* (נבלה),[21] surely a disgrace, a *nᵉbālāh*
(from the Hebrew *nbl*) has never returned inside, to the place of safety,
of life, where the Levite and Ephraimite have remained all through
the night. Unlike Lot, the *pilegesh* has no divine messenger to bring
her back to the safe side of the door. One reading of the fate of the
pilegesh, then, is that she has been broken so that the final boundary,
the דלת ('door'), could hold firm and protect the Levite against shame
and death. She has collapsed on the death side of the door. Another
possibility is that her body was the boundary that stopped the mob
from committing rape—that is, rape of the Levite. Another woman
found on the wrong side of the door is Tamar. After raping her, Amnon called to his servants, 'Put this woman out of my presence, and
bolt the door after her' (2 Sam. 13.18). The door becomes the marker
between security and danger, honor and shame, life and death.

In a lucid synchronic reading that links Genesis 19 and Judges 19–
20, Niditch observes that a homosexual rape would have been worse

20. S. Niditch, *War in the Hebrew Bible: A Study of the Ethics of Violence* (New
York: Oxford University Press, 1993), pp. 69-71. I do not claim to reflect the narrator's understanding of 'tribe', nor his view of the situation between the tribe of
Benjamin and the other tribes. Niditch notes that the *ḥērem* is considered as appropriate form of aggression only against outsiders. 'When the ban is used as a technique "to keep ingroup miscreants in line by a nervous and insecure leadership
with the power to enforce its will", it becomes divisive' (p. 70) Clearly this is the
situation in Judg. 21. Niditch shares my puzzlement over the designation of tribe
in this context, and the situation of exogamous marriage, neither of which has
much historical evidence. I suggest that the story does not function historically,
but rather serves to suppress the homosexuality in Judg. 19 as well as the violent
rape in Judg. 21.
21. The noun *nᵉbālāh*, defined in BDB as 'disgraceful folly', 'to do a thing
disgraceful according to Israel's standards', is used in conjunction with all the
biblical rape narratives; in Judg. 19.24 the term may refer to the threat of homosexual rape; in Judg. 20.6 the term clearly refers to the gang rape of the *pilegesh*, in
Gen. 34, 7 of the rape of Dinah. For further discussion of the term *nᵉbālāh* see Keefe,
'Rapes of Women', p. 82.

than the rape of the *pilegesh*, in the eyes of Israel, and ethically inde-
fensible.[22] Niditch does not, however, address the absence of anger or
moral outrage on the part of the narrator. Nor does she explain the
rage of the Levite in the following chapter of Judges. Perhaps the
biblical narrator has slammed the door on sodomy so effectively that
no reader, even a modern one, dares to press up against that door.
Like Lot and the Levite, who are exonerated for offering women as
substitutions, the reader is exonerated for not wondering if perhaps
the Levite had not been the victim after all. But the misreading
demands the answers to two crucial questions. Why else the Levite's
extraordinary rage? Why else the cutting up of the sacrificial victim?[23]
One must account for the Levite transforming the Benjaminites' threat
to sodomize him into a desire to kill him. The shame and horror of
sodomy were equivalent to death. Unruly unlawful male sexuality
according to the tale as used in Genesis does result in the death of the
Sodomites. But the Levite has eluded death. He escapes punishment
over her dead body. The Levite further vilifies the dead female body
by using it to incite his countrymen. Choosing to misread the sign of
her body, the men exact revenge on Benjamin. But then, in order to
assuage the guilt and anger against their brothers, they amplify the
violence done to one woman by violating many women. Each act of
violence is justified by hiding the truth behind the door, throwing out
lies to distract the spectators. Men's misreadings result in the mis-
treatment of women. The substitution of women for men occurs in
both the story of Judges 19 and in the revenge taken in Judges 21.
Gender inversion of the tale becomes the Levite's security.

While the violations of individual women in Genesis 19 and Judges
19–20 have become the subject of earnest debate in the feminist community, the carrying off of the women of Shiloh has been met with
near silence. The representation of violence and pain of rape have
been lost in a welter of interpretations that talk about reuniting the
tribes of Israel, fighting a holy war in YHWH's name, assuring the
continuation of the tribe of Benjamin. Male and female commentators

---

22. Niditch, 'The "Sodomite" Theme'.

23. Many scholars have noted the similarity between the cutting up of the
pilegesh and Saul's cutting up of the yoke of oxen in 1 Sam. 11.5-7. In both narratives the pieces are sent to the tribes of Israel to incite them to battle. Niditch
('The "Sodomite" Theme', p. 371) sees the dismembered body as a part of the
division of the body politic. Reading through the gender code, Exum argues that
'by leaving her husband the woman makes a gesture of sexual autonomy, so threatening to patriarchal ideology that it requires her to be punished sexually in the
most extreme form' (*Frgamented Women*, p. 181).

alike seem to identify deeply with the portrait of female victimization expressed in the narratives of violence to one woman, but silence greets the genocidal brutalization of the women of Shiloh.

Breaking the Silence of the Women of Shiloh

Feminist criticism combines the personal and the political, and insists on a kind of self-consciousness that is explicit about the origins of one's projects and the position from which one speaks. Undermining the traditional academic boundaries between professional and subjective is an example of the interaction between personal and political. I suspect that it would be impossible for any woman to write about rape without becoming emotionally involved in the work.[24]

Because the biblical text remains silent about the young women of Shiloh, I shall describe some of the documented atrocities from the recent gynocidal actions in Bosnia. The parallel seems strong, for the recent atrocities were committed during an ethno–religious civil war, a war in which men's violence was inscribed upon women's bodies. In both situations there is the strong patriarchal association of the female body with territory, so that raping one and conquering the other come metaphorically to the same thing. For those readers clinging to the 'marriage' element of the Judges 21 text, let me add that what Allen calls 'enforced pregnancy'[25] was also practiced by the Christian Serbs, against Muslim women. The following testimony was offered by a survivor of the Susica camp in eastern Bosnia. The witness was testifying about several young women who had been selected (for enforced pregnancy):

24. For riveting descriptions of the scenes of horror in the Bosnia rape camps, see Radmila Manojlovic Zarkovic, with Fran Peavey (eds.), *I remember = Sjecam Se : Writings by Bosnian Women Refugees* (San Francisco: Aunt Lute Books, 1996). Note: The memoirs appear in the original Serbo-Croatian, along with English, Spanish and Italian. Also Hukanovic Rezak, *The Tenth Circle of Hell: A Memoir of Life In The Death Camps of Bosnia* (trans. Colleen London and Midhat Ridjanovic; ed. Ammiel Alcalay; New York: Basic Books, 1996). I recommend these works with the warning provided by Beverly Allen: 'A repetitive serial form may easily hook even a reader disgusted by the events the text relates into wondering at least what comes next. This scene was so horrible, can the next one possibly be worse? And so the reader may keep turning the pages, caught in spite of her or his revulsion in the formal pleasure of repetitive linear narrative' (Beverley Allen, *Rape Warfare: The Hidden Genocide in Bosnia–Herzegovina and Croatia* [Minneapolis: University of Minnesota Press, 1996], p. 32, 87). As I have noted above, this sort of narrative risks placing the reader in the position of voyeur.

25. Allen, *Rape Warfare*, p. 87.

They started selecting young women. The first was only 14, the second could have been 16 or 17... I knew them all, they were from Vlasenica... Then they started yelling, 'We want the Muslims to see what our seed is'. The women were never seen again... We know that Dragan Nikolic knows about it very well. That's what he did... He told us himself: 'I am the commander of the camp. I'm your God and you have no other God but me'.[26]

What I would like to suggest is that after reading rape accounts such as the one quoted above from the recent genocide in Bosnia, the reader will fill the gaps and silences in Judges 21 with the cries of the victims of ethnic/religious rape of massive proportions. As I have argued elsewhere,[27] we do not read in a linear fashion. Regardless of the order of one's reading, what is immediately apparent is that female readers will feel an emotional connection between the plight of the Muslim women of Bosnia and the virgins of Shiloh—if readers allow themselves to dwell upon that sliver of biblical narrative. I do not mean to imply that men will not feel horror at these atrocities, but I have searched all the traditional accounts of holy war in Israel, of war suborned by YHWH, of war won by YHWH, and nowhere is there a mention of the carrying off of the women of Shiloh as rape, or even a hint that such a deed might have been divinely sanctioned but *against their will*. Much like violence portrayed in cartoons, the carrying off of the dancing maidens is accomplished without pain, without struggle, without resistance. If the narrative were focalized even for a moment through the eyes of the victims, one would be required to appropriate the female body as a sign of the violator's power. But the women remain as passive signifiers; the biblical storyteller is not interested in representing their experience. Thus, the reader must inhabit the gap, the silence, and through the power of imagination break the silence of the women of Shiloh. To leave them in silence is gynocide.

26. M. Sells, *The Bridge Betrayed: Religion and Genocide in Bosnia* (Berkeley: University of California Press, 1996), p. 21.

27. Alice Bach, *Women, Seduction, and Betrayal in Biblical Narrativee* (Cambridge: Cambridge University Press, 1997).

BIBLIOGRAPHY

Auerbach, Erich, *Mimesis: The Representation of Reality in Western Literature* (trans. Willard Trask; New York: New York University Press, 1953).

Allen, Beverly, *Rape Warfare: The Hidden Genocide in Bosnia–Herzegovina and Croatia* (Minneapolis: University of Minnesota Press, 1996).

Assmann, J., *Das kulturelle Gedächtnis: Schrift, Erinnerung und politische Identität in frühen Hochkulturen* (Munich: Beck, 1992).

Auld, A. Graeme, *Joshua, Judges, Ruth* (Philadelphia: Westminster Press, 1984).

Bach, Alice, *Women, Seduction, and Betrayal in Biblical Narrative* (Cambridge: Cambridge University Press, 1997).

Bal, Mieke, *Murder and Difference: Gender, Genre, and Scholarship on Sisera's Death* (trans. M. Gumpert: Bloomington: Indiana University Press, 1988).

—*Death and Dissymetry: The Politics of Coherence in the Book of Judges* (Chicago: University of Chicago Press, 1988).

—'Speech Acts and Body Language in Judges', in Elaine Scarry (ed.), *Literature and the Body: Essays on Populations and Persons* (Baltimore: The Johns Hopkins University Press, 1988).

—*Lethal Love: Feminist Literary Readings of Biblical Love Stories* (Bloomington: Indiana University Press, 1987).

Bal, Mieke, (ed.) *Anti-Covenant: Counter-Reading Women's Lives in the Hebrew Bible* (JSOTSup, 81; Bible and Literature Series, 22; Sheffield: Almond Press, 1989).

Balz-Cochois, Helgard, *Inanna: Wesensbild und Kult einer unmütterlichen Göttin* (Gütersloh: Gerd Mohn, 1992).

Barthes, Roland, 'Striptease', in *idem*, *Mythologies* (New York: Hill & Wang), pp. 84-87.

Biale, Rachel, *Women and Jewish Law: An Exploration of Women's Issues in Halakhic Sources* (New York: Schocken Books, 1984).

Boling, R.G., *Judges: A New Translation with Introduction and Commentary* (AB, 6A; Garden City, NY: Doubleday, 1975).

Boyarin, D., *Carnal Israel: Reading Sex in Talmudic Culture* (The New Historicism: Studies in Cultural Poetics, 25; Berkeley: University of California Press, 1993).

Braulik, G., *Deuteronomium. II. Kap. 16; 18-34; 12* (NEB, 28; Würzburg: Echter Verlag, 1992).

Braun, C. von, 'Zur Bedeutung der Sexualbilder im rassistischen Antisemitismus', in Inge Stephan *et al.* (eds.), *Jüdische Kultur und Weiblichkeit in der Moderne* (Literatur–Kultur–Geschlecht: Studien zur Literatur und Kulturgeschichte. Große Reihe, 2; Cologne: Böhlau, 1994), pp. 23-49.

Brenner, A. and F. van Dijk-Hemmes, *On Gendering Texts: Female and Male Voices in the Hebrew Bible* (Biblical Interpretation Series, 1; Leiden: E.J. Brill, 1993).

Brenner, A., *The Israelite Woman: Social Role and Literary Type in Biblical Narrative* (The Biblical Seminar, 2; Sheffield: JSOT Press, 1985).

Brenner A. (ed.), *A Feminist Companion to Genesis* (The Feminist Companion to the Bible, 2; Sheffield: Sheffield Academic Press, 1993).

—*A Feminist Companion to Judges* (The Feminist Companion to the Bible, 4; Sheffield: Sheffield Academic Press, 1993).

Brion, Marcel, *The Bible in Art: Miniatures, Paintings, Drawings and Sculptures Inspired by the Old Testament* (London: Phaidon Press, 1956).

Bronfen, E., *Nur über ihre Leiche: Tod, Weiblichkeit und Ästhetik* (Munich: dtr, 1994).

Brooten, B., 'Konnten Frauen im alten Judentum die Scheidung betreiben? Überlegungen zu Mk 10, 11-12 und 1 Kor 7, 10-11', *EvT* 42 (1982), pp. 65-80.

Brownmiller, S., *Against our Will: Men, Women and Rape* (New York: Simon & Schuster, 1975).

Bucher, Francois, *The Pamplona Bibles: A Facsimile Compiled from Two Picture Bibles with Martyrologies Commissioned by K. Sancho el Fuerte of Navarra (1194–1234) Amiens Manuscript Latin 108 and Harburg M. S. 1, 2 lat. 4 ^ , 15*, I-II (New Haven: Yale University Press, 1970).

Budde, K., *Das Buch der Richter* (KHAT, 7; Freiburg, 1897).

Burney, C.F., *The Book of Judges* (repr. New York: Ktav, 1970).

Burns, E.J., 'Judith or Jael?', *CBQ* 16 (1955), pp. 12-14.

—'The Genealogy of Judith', *CBQ* 18 (1956), pp. 19-22.

Butting, K., *Die Buchstaben werden sich noch wundern: Innerbiblische Kritik als Wegweisung feministischer Hermeneutik* (Berlin: Alektor, 1993).

Chambers 20th Century Dictionary (ed. E.M. Kirkpatrick; Edinburgh: W. & R. Chambers, new edn, 1983).

Charlesworth, James H. (ed.), *The Old Testament Pseudepigrapha*, II (Garden City, NY: Doubleday, 1985).

The Chronicles of Jeraḥmeel; or, The Hebrew Bible Historiale (trans. M. Gaster; New York: Ktav, 1971).

Clines, D.J.A., 'What Does Eve Do to Help and Other Irredeemably Androcentric Orientations in Genesis 1–3', in D.J.A. Clines, *What Does Eve Do to Help? And Other Readerly Questions to the Old Testament* (JSOTSup, 94; Sheffield: JSOT Press, 1990), pp. 25-48.

Cockerell, Sydney C., *Old Testament Miniatures: A Medieval Picture Book with 283 Paintings From the Creation to the Story of David* (New York: George Braziller, 1969).

Craghan, J.F., 'Esther, Judith and Ruth: Paradigms of Human Liberation', *BTB* 1 (1982), pp. 11-19.

—*Esther, Judith, Tobit, Jonah, Ruth* (OTM, 16; Wilmington, DE: Michael Glazier, 1982).

Craven, T., 'Tradition and Convention in the Book of Judith', in A. Loades (ed.), *Feminist Theology: A Reader* (Louisville, KY: Westminster/John Knox Press, 1990), pp. 29-41.

—*Artistry and Faith in the Book of Judith* (SBLDS, 7; Chico, CA: Scholars Press, 1983).

Cundall, A.E., *Judges: An Introduction and Commentary* (TOTC: London: Tyndale Press, 1966).

Curran, Leo, 'Rape and Rape Victims in the Metamorphoses', *Arethusa* 2 (1978), pp. 213-41.

Dancy, J.C., *The Shorter Books of the Apocrypha* (CNEB; Cambridge: Cambridge University Press, 1972).

DeLauretis, Teresa, 'The Violence of Rhetoric: Considerations on Representation and Gender', in *idem, Technologies of Gender* (Bloomington: Indiana University Press, 1987).

Dijk-Hemmes, F. van, 'Traces of Women's Texts in the Hebrew Bible', in A. Brenner and F. van Dijk-Hemmes, *On Gendering Texts: Female and Male Voices in the Hebrew Bible* (Biblical Interpretation Series, 1; Leiden: E.J. Brill, 1993), pp. 17-109.

Dimen, Muriel, 'Power, Sexuality, and Intimacy', in Alison Jagger and Susan Bordo (eds.), *Gender/Body/Knowledge* (New Brunswick: Rutgers University Press, 1989).

Donzelli, Carlo, *I Pittori Veneti del Settecento* (Florence: G. C. Sansoni, 1957).

The Doré Bible Gallery Containing One Hundred Superb Illustrations and a Page of Explanatory Letter-Press Facing Each: Illustrated by Gustave Doré (Philadelphia: Henry Altemus, 1890).

The Doré Bible Illustrations: 241 Illustrations by Gustave Doré (intro. Millicent Rose; New York: Dover Publications, 1974).

Ebach, Jürgen, 'Der Gott des Alten Tesaments—ein Gott der Rache? Versuch der Klärung einer gerade von Christen immer wieder gestellten Frage', *JK* 3 (1994), pp. 130-39.

Ebach, Jürgen, 'Der Gott des Alten Testaments—ein Gott der Rache?', in *idem, Biblische Erinnerungen: Theologische Reden zur Zeit* (Bochum: SWI, 1993), pp. 81-93.

Elder, L.B., 'Judith', in E. Schüssler Fiorenza (ed.), *Searching the Scriptures*. II. *A Feminist Commentary* (London: SCM Press, 1995).

Elman, Yaakov, *The Living Nach: Early Prophets* (Jerusalem: Moznaim, 1994).

Engel, H., ' "Der HERR ist ein Gott, der die Kriege zerschlägt": Zur griechischen Originalsprache und der Struktur des Buches Judith', in K.-D. Schunk and M. Augustin (eds.), *Goldene Apfel in silbernen Schafen* (BEAT, 20; Frankfurt am Main: Peter Lang, 1992), pp. 155-68.

—'Das Buch Judith', in E. Zenger (ed.), *Einleitung in das Alte Testament* (Stuttgart: Kohlhammer, 1995), pp. 192-200.

Enslin, M.S., *The Book of Judith* (Jewish Apocryphal Literature, 7; Leiden: E.J. Brill, 1972).

Exodus (ed. J.M. Wevers; Septuagint, II.1; Göttingen: Vandenhoek & Ruprecht, 1991).

Exum, J.C., *Plotted, Shot, and Painted: Cultural Representations of Biblical Women* (JSOTSup, 215; Gender, Culture, Theory, 3; Sheffield: Sheffield Academic Press, 1996).

—*Fragmented Women: Feminist (Sub)versions of Biblical Narratives* (JSOTSup, 163; Sheffield: JSOT Press, 1993).

—'Samson's Women', in *idem, Fragmented Women: Feminist (Sub)versions of Biblical Narratives* (JSOTSup, 163; Sheffield: JSOT Press, 1993).

—'Murder They Wrote', in Alice Bach (ed.), *The Pleasure of her Text* (Philadelphia: Trinity Press International, 1990), pp. 45-67.

—'The Theological Dimension of the Samson Saga', *VT* 23.1 (1983), pp. 30-45.

Fewell, D.N., 'Deconstructive Criticism: Achsah and the (E)razed City of Writing',
    in Gale A. Yee (ed.), *Judges and Method: New Approaches in Biblical Studies*
    (Minneapolis: Fortress Press, 1995), pp. 119-45.
—'Judges', in C.A. Newsom and Sharon H. Ringe (eds.), *The Women's Bible
    Commentary* (London: SPCK; Louisville, KY: Westminster/John Knox Press,
    1992), pp. 67-77.
Fewell, Danna Nolan, and David M. Gunn, *Gender, Power and Promise: The Subject
    of the Bible's First Story* (Nashville: Abingdon Press, 1993).
Foucault, Michel, *Power/Knowledge; Selected Interviews and Other Writings 1972–1977*
    (ed. and trans. Colin Gordon; New York: Pantheon Books, 1980).
Freedman, H., 'Joshua: A Introduction and Commentary', in A. Cohen (ed.), *Joshua
    and Judges* (London: Soncino, 1959), pp. xi-xvii.
Frymer-Kensky, T., 'Law and Philosophy: The Case of Sex in the Bible', *Semeia* 45
    (1989), pp. 90-102.
Gardner, A.E., 'The Song of Praise in Judith 16, 2-17 (LXX 16, 1-17)', *HeyJ* (1988),
    pp. 413-22.
Gilman, S.L., *Rasse, Sexualität und Seuche: Stereotypen aus der Innenwelt der westlichen
    Kultur* (Reinbek bei Hamburg: Rowohet, 1992).
Ginzberg, Louis, *The Legends of the Jews*, IV (Philadelphia: Jewish Publication Soci-
    ety of America, 1913).
Görg, Manfred, *Richter* (NEB; Würzburg: Echter Verlag, 1993).
Gravdal, Kathryn, *Ravishing Maidens: Writing Rape in Medieval French Literature and
    Law* (Philadelphia: University of Pennsylvania Press, 1991).
Griffin, Susan, *Rape: The Politics of Consciousness* (San Francisco: Harper & Row,
    1986).
—*Pornography and Silence: Culture's Revenge Against Nature* (New York: Harper &
    Row, 1981).
Haag, E., *Studien zum Buch Judith: Seine theologische Bedeutung und literarische
    Eigenart* (Trierer theologische Studien, 16; Trier: Paulinus, 1963).
Hamlin, E. John, *At Risk in the Promised Land: A Commentary on the Book of Judges*
    (Edinburgh: Handsel Press, 1990).
Hampson, D., *Theology and Feminism* (Signposts in Theology; Oxford: Basil Black-
    well, 1990).
Harris, Trudier, *Exorcising Blackness: Historical and Literary Lynching and Burning
    Rituals* (Bloomington: Indiana University Press, 1984).
Harrison, Beverly Wildung, 'The Power of Anger in the Work of Love: Christian
    Ethics for Women and Other Strangers', in *idem, Making the Connections: Essays
    in Feminist Social Ethics* (ed. Carol S. Robb; Boston: Beacon Press, 1985), pp. 3-
    21.
Heine, Susanne, 'Die feministische Diffamierung der Juden', in Kohn-Ley and
    Korotin (eds.), *Der feministische 'Sündenfall'?*, pp. 15-59.
Hellmann, M., *Judit—eine Frau im Spannungsfeld von Autonomie und göttlicher
    Führung: Studie über eine Frauengestalt des Alten Testaments* (Frankfurt am
    Main: Peter Lang, 1992).
Henten, J.W. van, 'Judith as Alternative Leader: A Rereading of Judith 7–13', in
    A. Brenner (ed.), *A Feminist Companion to Esther, Judith and Susanna* (The
    Feminist Companion to the Bible, 7; Sheffield: Sheffield Academic Press,
    1995), pp. 224-52.

Hertzberg, Hans Wilhelm, *Die Bücher Josua, Richter, Ruth* (ATD, 9; Göttingen: Vandenhoeck & Ruprecht, 1953).

Heschel, S., 'Konfigurationen des Patriarchats, des Judentums und des Nazismus im deutschen feministischen Denken', in Kohn-Ley and Korotin (eds.), *Der feministische 'Sündenfall'?*, pp. 160-84.

The Illustrated Bartsch (gen. ed. Walter L. Strauss; New York: Abaris Books, 1978–92).

Jahnow, Hedwig, *et al.* (eds.), *Feministische Hermeneutik und Erstes Testament: Analysen und Interpretationen* (Stuttgart: W. Kohlhammer, 1994).

Jones-Warsaw, K., 'Toward a Womanist Hermeneutic: A Reading of Judges 19–21', in Brenner (ed.), *A Feminist Companion to Judges*, pp. 172-86.

Josephus, *Jewish Antiquities, Vol. 5, Books V–VIII* (trans. H. Thackeray and Ralph Marcus; London: Heinemann, 1966).

Jüngling, H.-W., *Richter 19: Ein Plädoyer für das Königtum. Stilistische Analyse der Tendenzerzählung Ri 19, 1-30a; 21,25* (AB, 84; Rome: Biblical Institute, 1981).

Kaiser, Otto *et al* (eds.), *Texte aus der Umwelt des Alten Testamentes. II. Orakel, Rituale, Bau- und Votivinschriften, Lieder und Gebete* (Gütersloh: Gerd Mohn, 1986–91).

Keefe, Alice, 'Rapes of Women/Wars of Men', *Semeia* 61 (1993), pp. 79-97.

Kellenbach, K. von, *Anti-Judaism in Feminist Religious Writings* (American Academy of Religion Cultural Criticism Series, 1; Atlanta, GA: Scholars Press, 1994).

Kirschbaum, Engelbert, *Lexicon der christlichen Ikonographie*, II (ed. Günther Bandmann and Wolfgang Branfels; Rome: Herder, 1970).

Klein, Lillian R., 'Honor and Shame in Esther', in A. Brenner (ed.), *A Feminist Companion to Esther, Judith and Susanna* (The Feminist Companion to the Bible, 7; Sheffield: Sheffield Academic Press, 1995), pp. 149-75.

—'A Spectrum of Female Characters in the Book of Judges', in Brenner (ed.), *A Feminist Companion to Judges*, pp. 24-33.

—'The Book of Judges: Paradigm and Deviation in Images of Women', in Brenner (ed.), *A Feminist Companion to Judges*, pp. 55-71.

—*The Triumph of Irony in the Book of Judges* (Sheffield: Sheffield Academic Press, 1988).

Kohn-Ley, C., and Ilse Korotin (eds.), *Der feministische 'Sündenfall'? Antisemitische Vorurteile in der Frauenbewegung* (Vienna: Picus, 1994).

Kolodny, Annette, 'Dancing in the Minefields: Some Observations on the Theory, Practice and Politics of A Feminist Literary Criticism'; reprinted in R. Warhol and D. Herndl (eds.), *Feminisms: An Anthology of Literary Theory and Criticism* (New Brunswick: Rutgers University Press, 1993 [1980]).

Kooij, A. van der, 'On Male and Female Views in Judges 4 and 5', in B. Becking and M. Dijkstra (eds.), *On Reading Prophetic Texts: Gender-specific and Related Studies in Memory of Fokkelien van Dijk-Hemmes* (Biblical Interpretation Series, 18; Leiden: E.J. Brill, 1996), pp. 135-52.

Levine, A.J., 'Sacrifice and Salvation: Otherness and Domestication in the Book of Judith', in J.C. VanderKam (ed.), *'No One Spoke Ill of Her': Essays on Judith* (SBL Early Judaism and its Literature, 2; Atlanta: Scholars Press, 1992), pp. 17-30; reprinted in A. Brenner (ed.), *A Feminist Companion to Esther, Judith and Susanna* (The Feminist Companion to the Bible, 7; Sheffield: Sheffield Academic Press, 1995), pp. 209-23.

Lipman, Jean, and Alice Winchester, *The Flowering of American Folk Art: 1776–1876* (New York: Viking, 1974).

Mathys, H.-P., *Dichter und Beter: Theologen aus spätalttestamentlicher Zeit* (OBO, 132; Freiburg: Universitätsverlag; Göttingen: Vandenhoeck & Ruprecht, 1994).

Maus, Cynthia Pearl, *The Old Testament and the Fine Arts: An Anthology of Pictures, Poetry, Music, and Stories Covering the Old Testament* (New York: Harper & Brothers, 1954).

McKay, H., 'On the Future of Feminist Biblical Criticism', in Brenner and Fontaine (eds.), *A Feminist Companion to Reading the Bible*, pp. 61-83.

Meyers, C. *Discovering Eve: Ancient Israelite Women in Context* (Oxford: Oxford University Press, 1988).

Midrash Tanḥuma (Jerusalem: Lewin-Epstein, 1964).

Midrash Tanḥuma Sefer Vayikra (Williamsburg: Me'ein Ha-Torah, 1963).

Milne, P.J., 'Toward Feminist Companionship: The Future of Biblical Studies and Feminism', in A. Brenner and C. Fontaine (eds.), *A Feminist Companion to Reading the Bible: Approaches, Methods and Strategies* (Sheffield: Sheffield Academic Press, 1997), pp. 39-60.

—'No Promised Land: Rejecting the Authority of the Bible', in H. Shanks (ed.), *Feminist Approaches to the Bible* (Washington, DC: Biblical Archaeology Society, 1995), pp. 47-73.

—'What Shall We Do with Judith? A Feminist Reassessment of a Biblical "Heroine" ', *Semeia* 62 (1993), pp. 37-58.

Moore, Carey A., *Judith: A New Translation with Introduction and Commentary* (AB, 40; Garden City, NY: Doubleday, 1985).

Mosca, Paul, G., 'Who Seduced Whom? A Note on Joshua 15:18//Judges 1:14', *CBQ* 45.1 (1984), pp. 18-22.

Niditch, Susan, *War in the Hebrew Bible: A Study in the Ethics of Violence* (New York: Oxford University Press, 1993).

—'The "Sodomite" Theme in Judges 19–20: Family, Community, and Social Integration', *CBQ* 44 (1982), pp. 365-78.

Olivier, C., *Jokastes Kinder: Die Psyche der Frau im Schatten der Mutter* (Munich: dtr, 8th edn, 1993).

Pfister, Manfred, 'Konzepte der Intertextualität', in Ulrich Broich and Manfred Pfister (eds.), *Intertextualität: Formen, Funktionen, anglistische Fallstudien* (Konzepte der Sprach- und Literaturwissenschaft, 35; Tübingen: Niemeyer, 1985), pp. 1-30.

Pigler, A. *Barockthemen: Eine Auswahl von Verzeichnissen zur Ikonographie des 17. und 18. Jahrhunderts*, II (3 vols.; Budapest: Academiai Kiado, 2nd edn, 1974).

Poethig, Eunice B., 'The Victory Song Tradition of the Women of Israel' (PhD dissertation; New York University, 1985).

Polain, M. Lois, *Catalogue des livres imprimés au quinzième siècle des bibliothèques de Belgique* (4 vols.; Brussels Société des Bibliophiles et Iconophiles de Belgique, 1932).

Priebatsch, Hans Yohanan, 'Das Buch Judith und seine hellenistischen Quellen', *ZDPV* 90 (1974), pp. 50-60.

Rad, Gerhard von, *Gottes Wirken in Israel: Vorträge zum Alten Testament* (ed. Odil Hannes Steck; Neukirchen–Vluyn: Neukirchener Verlag, 1974).

—*Der heilige Krieg im alten Israel* (Zürich: Zwingli, 1951).

Rashkow, I., *The Phallacy of Genesis: A Feminist-Psychoanalytic Approach* (Literary Currents in Biblical Interpretation: Louisville, KY: Westminster/John Knox Press, 1993).

Rich, Adrienne, 'When We Dead Waken: Writing as Revision'; reprinted in Barbara Charlesworth and Albert Gelpi (eds.), *Adrienne Rich's Poetry* (New York: W.W. Norton, 1975 [1972]).

Rosenberg, A.J. (ed.), *Judges: A New Translation* (New York: The Judaica Press, 1987).

Scarry, Elaine, *The Body in Pain: The Making and Unmaking of the World* (New York: Oxford University Press, 1985).

Schaumberger, C., '"Das Recht, anders zu sein, ohne dafür bestraft zu werden": Rassismus als Problem weißer feministischer Theologie', in C. Schaumberger (ed.), *Weil wir nicht vergessen wollen...zu einer feministischen Theologie im deutschen Kontext* (AnFragen, 1; Münster: Morgana-Fraüenbuch Verlag, 1987), pp. 101-22.

Schmidt, T., '*Auf das Opfer darf keiner sich berufen': Opferdiskurse in der öffentlichen Diskussion zu sexueller Gewalt gegen Mädchen* (Bielefeld: Kläue, 1996).

Schuller, Eileen M., 'The Apocrypha', in Carol A. Newsom and Sharon H. Ringe (eds.), *The Women's Bible Commentary* (London: SPCK, 1992), pp. 234-43.

Schüssler Fiorenza, E., *But She Said: Feminist Practices Of Biblical Interpretation* (Boston: Beacon Press, 1992).

—*In Memory of Her: A Feminist Theological Reconstruction of Christian Origins* (New York: Crossroad, 1983).

Schwienhorst-Schönberger, L., '"...denn ihr seid Fremde gewesen im Lande Ägypten": Zur sozialen und rechtlichen Stellung von Fremden und Ausländern im alten Israel', *BiLi* 2 (1990), pp. 108-17.

Searles, Patricia, and Ronald J. Berger (eds.), *Rape and Society: Readings on the Problem of Sexual Assault* (Boulder, CO: Westview Press, 1995).

Sell, H.T., *Studies of Famous Bible Women* (New York: Fleming H. Revelle, 1925).

Sells, Michael, *The Bridge Betrayed: Religion and Genocide in Bosnia* (Berkeley: University of California Press, 1996).

Shekan, P.W., 'The Hand of Judith', *CBQ* 25 (1963), pp. 94-110.

Siegele-Wenschkewitz, L., 'Rassismus, Antisemitismus, Sexismus', *Schlangenbrut* 43 (1993), pp. 15-18.

Smend, R., *Yahweh War and Tribal Confederation* (Nashville: Abingdon Press, 1970).

Smith, C., 'Samson and Delilah: A Parable of Power?', *JSOT* 76 (1997), pp. 45-57.

Soggin, J. Alberto, *Judges: A Commentary* (trans. John Bowden; Philadelphia: Westminster Press, 1981).

Sölle, D., J.H. Kirchberger and H. Haag, *Great Women of the Bible in Art and Literature* (trans. J.H. Kirchberger; Grand Rapids, MI: Eerdmans, 1993).

Sorge, Elga, *Religion und Frau: Weibliche Spiritualität im Christentum* (Stuttgart: W. Kohlhammer, 1985).

Sparrow, W. Shaw, *The Old Testament in Art: From the Creation of the World to the Death of Moses. II. Joshua to Job. Being a Continuation of the Old Testament in Art* (London: Hodder & Stoughton, n.d.).

Spieckermann, Hermann, *Heilsgegenwart: Eine Theologie der Psalmen* (FRLANT, 148; Göttingen: Vandenhoek & Ruprecht, 1989).

Strathausen, A., *Ver-gewalt-igung: Zu Soziologie und Recht sexueller Machtverhältnisse* (Münster: DVV, 1989).

Swete, H.B. (ed.), *Judges* (OTG, 1; Cambridge: Cambridge University Press, 1925).

Thürmer-Rohr, C., 'Frauen in Gewaltverhältnissen zur Generalisierung des Opfer-begriffs', in Studienschwerpunkt 'Frauenforschung', am Institut für Sozial-pädagogik der TU Berlin (ed.), *Mittäterschaft und Entdeckungslust* (Berlin: Orlanda Fräuenbuch Verlag, 1990).

Tischler, N., *Legacy of Eve: Women of the Bible* (Atlanta: John Knox Press, 1977).

Trible, P., *Texts of Terror: Literary-Feminist Readings of Biblical Narratives* (Philadelphia: Fortress Press, 1984).

—*God and the Rhetoric of Sexuality* (Overtures to Biblical Theology; Philadelphia: Fortress Press, 1978).

—'Bringing Miriam out of the Shadows', in Athalya Brenner (ed.), *A Feminist Companion to Exodus to Deuteronomy* (The Feminist Com;panion to the Bible, 6; Sheffield: Shefield Academic Press, 1994), pp. 166-86.

—'If the Bible's so Patriarchal, How Come I Love It?', *BR* 8.5 (1992), pp. 44-47, 55.

Turner, Jane, (ed.), *The Dictionary of Art*, I (34 vols.; London: Macmillan, 1996).

Veerkamp, T., 'Die Bibel: ein "fremdes Buch"', in Wagner *et al.* (eds.), *(Anti-) Rassistische Irritationen*, pp. 21-24

Wacker, Marie-Theres, 'Gefährliche Erinnerungen: Feministische Blicke auf die hebräische Bibel', in M.-T. Wacker (ed.), *Theologie feministisch: Disziplinen, Schwerpunkte, Richtungen* (Düsseldorf: Patmos, 1988), pp. 14-58.

Wagner, Silvia *et al.* (eds.), *(Anti-)Rassistische Irritationen: Biblische Texte und interkulturelle Zusammenarbeit* (Berlin: Alektor, 1994).

Weigel, S., *Topographien der Geschlechter* (Kulturgeschichtliche Studien zur Literatur: Reinbek bei Hamburg: Rowohlt, 1990).

Weinfeld, M., 'Divine Intervention in War in Ancient Israel and the Ancient Near east', in H. Tadmor and M. Weinfeld (eds.), *History, Historiography and Interpretation* (Jerusalem: Magnes Press, 1983).

Westermann, C., *Das Loben Gottes in der Psalmen* (Göttingen: Vandenhoeck & Ruprecht, 1954).

White, Sidney Ann, 'In the Steps of Jael and Deborah: Judith as Heroine', in James C. VanderKam (ed.), *'No One Spoke Ill of Her': Essays on Judith* (SBL Early Judaism and its Literature, 2; Atlanta: Scholars Press, 1992), pp. 5-16.

Wilson, Nancy, *Our Tribe: Queer Folks, God, Jesus, and the Bible* (San Francisco: HarperCollins, 1995).

Witvliet, T., 'Rassismus und Eurozentrismus: Historische Einblicke', in Wagner *et al.* (eds.), *(Anti-)Rassistische Irritationen*, pp. 189-200.

Wurtzel, E., *Bitch: In Praise of Difficult Women* (London: Quartet Books; New York: Doubleday, 1998).

Yee, Gale A. (ed.), *Judges and Method: New Approaches in Biblical Studies* (Minneapolis: Fortress Press, 1995), pp. 131-32

Yerushalmi, Samuel, *The Book of Judges: Me'am Lo'ez* (Jerusalem: Moznaim, 1991).

Zampetti, Pietro, *Dal Ricci al Tiepolo: I Pittori di figura del Setticento a Venezia. Catalog della Mostra* (Venezia: Alfieri, Edizioni D'Arte, 1969).

Zenger, Erich, *Ein Gott der Rache? Feindpsalmen verstehen* (Freiburg: Herder, 1994); ET *A God of Vengeance?* (trans. Linda M. Maloney; Louisville, KY: Westminster/John Knox Press, 1996).

—'Wir erkennen keinen anderen als Gott an...' (Jdt. 8,20): Programm und Rele-
     vanz des Buches Judith', *RHS* 39.1 (1996), pp. 23-36.
—*Das Erste Testament: Die jüdische Bibel und die Christen* (Düsseldorf: Patmos, 3rd
     edn, 1993).
—'Judith/Judithbuch', in *TRE*, XVII, pp. 404-408.
—*Das Buch Judit* (JSHRZ, 1; Gütersloh: Gütersloher Verlagshaus, 1981).
—'Der Judithroman als Traditionsmodell des Jahweglaubens', *TTZ* 83 (1974),
     pp. 65-80.
—*Das Buch Exodus* (Düsseldorf: Patmos, 1978).

INDEXES

INDEX OF REFERENCES

OLD TESTAMENT

INDEX OF AUTHORS